VEGAN
RECIPES FROM
JAPAN

VEGAN
RECIPES FROM
JAPAN

—◇◇◇—

MALTE HÄRTIG
JULE FELICE FROMMELT

GRUB STREET | LONDON

CONTENTS

—◇—

INTRODUCTION

————◇◇◇————

From the very beginning we had the idea of creating a cookbook revolving around the seasons and with a special focus on vegetables and their beauty.

Jule is a photographer who lives with her family in Berlin. But whenever time allows, she can be found at the place where we cooked and photographed the food featured in this book: an island in the Spree Forest, near the town of Lübbenau. Jule is passionate about gardening. So this is how it came about. Jule could photograph dishes prepared using the vegetables she grew herself. What could be better than having a photographer who is also a gardener?

And together with Jule, I, Malte, devised, developed and cooked the dishes. This book tells our story and showcases the recipes resulting from it. I have a doctorate in philosophy and am also a trained chef with a passion for cooking. I spent more than a year and a half in Japan and studied the country's traditional and refined Kaiseki cuisine, as well as the tea ceremony and Zen Buddhism. The subject of Japan stems from this.

Japanese cuisine and the beauty of vegetables: we thought they made a wonderful combination. And so we made plans. Jule made a planting plan for her garden and looked for backgrounds for the photos and for suitable dishes.

The property on the Spree Forest island is home to old oak and fruit trees – including apple, mirabelle plum, cherry, plum and quince trees – in addition to two main houses that are being restored, a few *Datschen* – weekend retreats that are remnants of the former East Germany – scattered through the forest that are also awaiting renovation or restoration, a large meadow, a small landing for Spreewald barges, a tool shed and, most important of all, the vegetable garden. Many of the vegetables shown in the book came from the garden, but not all. Although we were guided by the seasons, we didn't slavishly limit ourselves to them. Moreover, we bought ingredients at organic and Asian food markets and locally in the area. We couldn't do without citrus fruits from the south of Europe. And incidentally, the round-grain rice we used came from Italy. Apart from the sake, only dry ingredients, such as seaweed and shiitake mushrooms, came from the Far East. Good-quality, firm silken tofu is now widely available. This allowed us to be true to our principle of letting ourselves be guided by the nature of things and taking them as they are.

Jule and I would go into the garden time and again, to smell, look at and taste the vegetables. We would take a few back with us to the kitchen and then ask them what they wanted to become. I did not go with a fixed set of already developed recipes. Most of them were created on the spot, the result of conversations and using intuition more than reasoning.

In a total of six stays and seven weeks over the space of six months, we cooked and photographed out there on the island, co-existing with some of the island's other inhabitants. These included the three other families with whom Jule and her family shared ownership of the property, the wild boar that grunted and rooted around the property at night, the herons and deer, birds and insects, the wind and weather, the rustling of the trees, the rampantly growing grass, the mice in the kitchen and the martens under the roof. And the *Fließe* – the name collectively given to the maze of canals that wind their way through the region – whose waters have been flowing quietly, contemplatively and somehow also wisely, every day, for a long time, and for a long time to come.

The only clear concept we came with was what we had taken from Zen, the Japanese tea ceremony and Kaiseki cuisine. Then we simply set off on our way. The route we took and what we found as we went along can be seen on the following pages, divided by the seasons into spring, summer, autumn and winter.

We hope you find this book interesting reading and enjoy cooking the dishes we present.

Jule Felice Frommelt and Malte Härtig

OUR PHILOSOPHY OF ZEN

―◇◇◇―

WHAT IS ZEN?

Zen Buddhism espouses the idea that enlightenment is possible, either suddenly and spontaneously, or gradually through practice and through various stages of attainment. This has led to the development of the different schools and traditions of Zen.

For our needs, we should explain Zen in general terms. The basic assumption of Zen is that there is a path or way to enlightenment that should be followed. This led to the development in Japan of the 'way arts', such as calligraphy, archery and the famous tea ceremony.

Following a path that leads to enlightenment is for us the equivalent of having an insight into the nature of things, namely of seeing and understanding that things are what they are. However, this does not mean that they can't be fashioned. In fact, carrots and celery, for example, invite us to engage with them, with their essence, their beauty, their being. To cook them, eat them and, to a certain extent, become carrot and celery ourselves when we chew and digest them and absorb their energy. We cook with vegetables in this book because we love vegetables. And because we love life.

The German physicist Thomas Vilgis, who is very interested in food and its molecular properties, once said something very similar from a physical perspective: things are what they are. At the molecular level, our preparation techniques would change very little of the basic structure of these things.

Our Zen philosophy deals with the essentials and therefore the essence of things. Cooking is a form of knowledge about the world. And so is food. But cooking is also a practice. Through the specific actions of preparing, cutting, cooking and subsequent eating, we come into contact with vegetables and grains. But we, and our need for food, are also the reason to plant new carrots. At best, we absorb their energy, so it is not lost; it was not in vain. Things change shape; they transform. Cooking and eating are transformation processes, and at the same time they are processes of encounter, interaction and exchange of energy.

For the Zen master Dogen Zenji (1200–1253), aside from seated meditation without thinking, every form of engagement in activity was an exercise on the path to enlightenment. He also set out what he saw as responsibilities in the kitchen when he wrote his rules for monastic life. *Instructions for the Cook* is one of his most famous treatises. It contains the notion that the head cook of a monastery, by being in charge of the kitchen, should have the second highest rank in the monastery and be a role model and master. This was because he was responsible for feeding the other monks every day and was therefore responsible for their lives. Such a task could not be valued highly enough. In this way, the head cook of the monastery made a significant contribution to enabling the monks to follow the path to enlightenment. Consequently, according to Dogen, he should provide them only with the essentials. Not too much. And not too little. Just enough. People in Japan say that you shouldn't eat until you're full, only until you're satisfied. And we think the same way. It's about quality over quantity. One particular Japanese saying goes: 'Eat until you're eighty per cent full.' You should try this some time. This isn't something we are brought up with in the West.

As frugal as Zen food sounds, it also always showed the path to enlightenment taken by the monastery cook. For instance, in the way rice was carefully sorted, washed and cooked, it became clear to Dogen that the cook had his attention focused only on the here and now, on what he was doing, and that he had his eye trained on every single grain of rice. Dogen advised the monastery cook to care for it as if it were his own eyes, and if he were to find grains of sand in the rice, the sand should not be seen as inferior to the grains of rice. 'See both', said Dogen, 'and throw them both away at the same time, sand and rice.'

This sounds strange to us. However, behind it lie two essential tenets of Zen: All things have their value. All things are incomparable.

Such principles teach us a certain attitude towards the world. And our attitudes are what ultimately shape our actions. The attitude of the monastery cook – and of any other cook – can be read in the plate or bowl of food that they serve. Were things handled carefully? Was the essence of the food recognised and its potential developed or not?

Dogen defined what a good meal should be like, guided by the Chinese philosophy of the five elements. There should be five colours: red, yellow, green, white and black or purple; and five preparation methods: simmered, steamed, grilled, fried and raw. And six tastes should be included: sweet, sour, salty, bitter, spicy and mild. The Chinese refer to mild as bland, and appreciate it as a sign of high quality food. In Japan, one would perhaps also say 'restrained'. The culinary form of 'restrained' is the famous dashi and the invisibly abundant use made of it, which we will deal with later.

According to Dogen, the monastery meal should express three qualities. It should be light and soft, clean and fresh, and show precision and meticulousness. And the cook should be instilled with three attitudes during the preparation: with a joyful heart, which goes hand in hand with the gratitude of being allowed to cook for others, and thus follow the path of the Buddha; with a motherly heart, showing the care that parents have for their own children; and a vast heart, one that is as steadfast as a mountain and as open as the sea. If this is borne in mind, a harmonious and good meal will come into being as if by itself.

These instructions led to the development of a cuisine, known as Shojin Ryori. Shojin means mind and advancement and therefore denotes the Zen Buddhist path to enlightenment through practice. Ryori means cuisine or a style of cooking. Shojin Ryori is a very special cuisine. It is light, refined, tasteful and highly aesthetic, and vegan. It makes you feel satisfied and sometimes even happy because it is light on the stomach and provides positive energy. And best of all, because it's cooked with love. If you should encounter Shojin Ryori in Japan or elsewhere, make the most of the opportunity. It can be a unique experience. Shojin Ryori is an extraordinary way to nourish body, soul and spirit alike and very gracefully.

This cuisine and the guiding principles set out by Zen master Dogen were the starting point for our cookbook. They were the first thoughts with which we started out on our path. But we are not in Japan, and we aren't in a Zen Buddhist monastery. Most of us aren't likely to be full-time chefs whose way of cooking is at the same time their path to enlightenment and, therefore, whole purpose in life, even if sometimes one might wish this were the case. As a result, a question began to take shape with every step we took: how can we convey this, or rather, what thoughts will we take from all this and present here to the non-Japanese-speaking world?

We tried implementing all of Dogen's rules, but it led us away from our basic premise. Finally, we have reduced it all down to the essence, which can be summarised in a single sentence by the famous tea master Sen no Rikyu (1522–1591) that actually refers to the traditional tea ceremony. When asked whether the use of fine and elegant utensils was suitable for the simple act of drinking tea alone, he replied: 'Let us act in accordance with its nature; that is the true way of tea'. In the context of our book and in our lifestyle, that means: 'let's take things as they are'. We'll also be looking at this point in more detail later.

COOKING IS CUTTING

Japanese cooks sometimes say this modestly, almost humbly. By this they mean that their fundamental activity is actually the cutting of food. On the one hand, this is because food of very high quality is actually delivered to the restaurant by farmers, fishermen and producers and it *only* really has to be cut into shape. This notion, however, also ties in with what was explained previously: things are what they are – even if Western chefs sometimes present themselves and their food very differently – and even with lots of razzle-dazzle, foams, spherification and so on, we can only marginally change them. On the other hand, the motto 'cooking is cutting' focuses attention on the actual moment the cutting is performed: on the experience, practice and mastery of wielding a knife; on the knife itself, and through it, on the smith; just as it does on the cook, and on the vegetables or fish, because cutting has a direct effect on their taste, on their firmness or softness, juiciness or dryness, on their ability to be picked up with chopsticks and to be chewed in the mouth. And naturally on appearance, on the beauty of things (see the example of the rainbow chard on page 32 and the parsnip on page 170). Cutting contains all this and more. It is perhaps the most crucial moment of cooking. And yet, it all too often seems routine and banal. We need only look at the knives in our kitchen drawers and at their quality for proof.

Japanese cuisine is basically a simple cuisine. Ingredients are prepared using simple techniques: grilled, fried, pickled and raw, steamed and simmered, which is exactly the way Dogen recommended to the monastery chef. We have also been guided by this. Consequently, the dishes in this book are structured by these techniques.

Furthermore, the dishes follow the seasons, resulting in the four chapters: Spring, Summer, Autumn and Winter. And we loosely based ourselves on the Kaiseki menu.

Kaiseki cuisine is the equivalent of haute cuisine in Japan. Its origin lies in the tea ceremony and in tea master Rikyu's belief that if there is food to accompany the tea, it should precede the tea and be given less importance than the tea. And there should be a token quantity that will prevent starvation. Kaiseki can be translated as 'stone in the robe', a reference to the monks in Zen monasteries who are said to have placed hot stones in the folds of their robes near their stomachs to ward off hunger and cold during *zazen*, seated meditation, allowing them to fully clear their minds.

Therefore, there are close connections between Zen, the tea ceremony and Kaiseki cuisine. So, what does all this mean? The answer is that we must involve ourselves with the things that are available to us.

THE WISDOM OF THINGS

You will by now have now noticed how the term 'things' has popped up quite a few times and perhaps you've given it some thought. Is it supposed to mean food? 'Things' sounds a lot like 'stuff', like screws, cables or roof racks. I had already thought long and deeply about this point when I was writing my doctoral thesis on simplicity in Japanese Kaiseki cuisine, and to this day I can think of no better term to express that 'things' as described above have their own worth. They're not just food, in the literal sense of substances that sustain our life. Although they are that too. And they're also not just 'ingredients' that are supposed to work together to make a dish. It's about the things themselves, the actual parsnip or the potato. Above all, it is because, in the sense of Zen, they're a part of this world; they're living beings like us, and for this reason alone they are worthy of respect.

There are some beautiful but confusing stories in the Zen tradition, such as one where a musician plays the harp and a master observes and ponders. Is the musician playing his instrument or, on the contrary, is it not the harp that is playing the musician and allowing him to make sound? Taken in our context, we could ask the following questions. Do we really cook the celery or does the celery not end up cooking us? Do we use the knife to cut the carrot? Does the knife cut the carrot? Or does the carrot cut us? Let's take it a step further: could the knife be cutting us when it is guiding our hand through the vegetables? Or does everything happen simultaneously in the end, depending on the way you look at it? 'The Wisdom of Things' is the title of an essay I wrote on this subject in the book *Philosophy of Cooking*.

So it's about things. Please forgive the use of this somewhat unusual word when it comes to peas and strawberries. But it's precisely this confusion about everyday things that is important to me, because it allows us to focus on the essence of things as we choose, cook and eat them.

SEASONING AS A PHILOSOPHY

As you can see, a deep wisdom is possible in even the simplest actions. Now we come to the subject of seasoning. Even if Japanese cuisine (as we also do) advises us to accept things according to their true nature, this does not mean that they cannot be altered and fashioned. It is only a question of *how* – how deeply I should try to penetrate the structure of things. Given that cooking is cutting, then the change is quite insignificant.

However, let's look at this in a more practical light. Essentially, there are actually only a handful of ingredients that are supposed to 'season' or simply add flavour without making their presence felt too strongly. First and foremost, this is the role played by dashi, which is followed by mirin and soy sauce, and sometimes sake and miso, as well as salt and sugar. That's it.

Again, the secret that comes into play is that everything is restricted to the essentials. Japanese cuisine has developed a theory of combinations, through which every food that you find during the course of the seasons can be enhanced by its own flavour. It's a bit like jazz: there are scales to guide the musician, which also form the basis from which an infinite number of variations can be spontaneously produced. They are connected by their transience. It is in the music you hear in a jazz club, or when that one specific carrot with its own particular shape and own particular flavour is placed in front of me.

Let's take things as they are.

What this means is the recipes in this cookbook, as in many Japanese cookbooks, require very little more than these ingredients.

Let's get down to details. Not all dashi is the same. There are countless variations. Classic dashi is a stock made using smoked and fermented bonito flakes, kombu kelp seaweed and water. The vegan dashi used in Zen monasteries is made using shiitake mushrooms and kombu. We use a pure kombu dashi, except when making dipping soup for soba noodles and dipping sauce for tempura.

Dashi can only work if it is as intensely flavoured as possible, given that it is made with so few ingredients. Which kombu is the best and when? Rishiri-kombu, produced in the Rishiri area of northern Hokkaido, is suited to refined soups. Ma-kombu, however, is more intense and elementary.

Because the ingredients are kept so simple, their quality shows through extremely clearly and unforgivingly. If you use a cheap mirin, which is mainly sugar, you won't enjoy the recipes in this book very much, whereas mirin from a wholefood shop is very suitable. There's a recently established business that puts a great deal of heart, soul and inspiration into making soy sauces, miso and similar products, such as sangohachi pickles, and even mirin. We used them almost exclusively. Even if the price is a little higher, your vegetables will show their gratitude, and you will also thank yourself, because you will be able to very discreetly coax the subtlest traces of goodness out of carrots and celery. Even a normal soy sauce from a whole food shop is like being hit by a steamroller in comparison. If this tip doesn't interest you, here's another that will: less is more. When it comes to seasoning, the Japanese Kaiseki chef knows that even a few too many grains of salt can change the flavour of food from exquisite to crude – and this also applies to the recipes in this book. When you season, the effect you should aim for is one of not having seasoned.

Seasoning is actually a philosophy; it is basically about not adding external flavours to the vegetables, or adding very little in the way to which we're accustomed. The idea is to bring out the flavours inherent to them through the use of amino acids, which are natural flavour enhancers. They are given roundness and body through the use of mirin and sugar, for a little sweetness, and sake, miso and soy sauce, for complexity.

Let's return to the subject of kombu and dashi. I still had a good supply of the Rishiri-kombu that I had bought during my 'field research' in Kyoto. And we had double-filtered soft water from the depth of the well.

The quality of the water should not be underestimated, because soft water allows the aromas and other components from the kombu to diffuse better. It's the same with tea. Soft water is better able to absorb the subtlest flavours. And every day it made me glad to find that they take their water very seriously even in the midst of an island in the Spree Forest.

The classic dashi made with smoked bonito flakes produces a clean umami taste that stimulates the entire oral cavity. However, that was not our intention. We also wanted to pare its taste down to its very essence so that we could clearly accentuate the basic flavours of the vegetables, which is why we chose to make pure kombu dashi using filtered water.

The simplest method for this is cold extraction overnight.

Soak 4 g kombu – Rishiri-kombu in our case – in 1 litre of water overnight. I was able to make my dashi even more quickly and more naturally on hot summer days. I had left the kombu to soak in the water on the work surface next to the chopping board at room temperature, and I noticed how the kombu released its taste into the water and the dashi developed its flavour after only a quarter of an hour. I was then able to work throughout the day with the dashi at that level of intensity.

Kombu has the highest natural level of glutamate of any food. When it comes to bringing out the intrinsic flavour of vegetables, glutamate is sometimes, but not always, essential. It works like a secret cutting technique or some sort of unseen manipulation. Both are critical in Japanese cuisine to bring out the essence of the daikon radish, for example. Working with Japanese seasonings is like building a stage on which vegetables can showcase their natural beauty and simplicity.

This again fits well with the basic premise of bringing out what's already there. Things are already *what* they are and *the way* they are when they land on the chopping board. And we have the wonderful opportunity and task to bring out their essence and to make it shine, 'no matter whether it is a very noble vegetable or a wilted lettuce leaf', in the words of Zen master Dogen. When a person cooks, a secret power unfolds that can't be grasped properly with the mind. I would describe it as love. For things, for guests and for oneself.

Cooking with love. That's the essence.

What is needed for this? In addition to the previously mentioned ingredients – water, kombu, mirin, sake, soy sauce, sugar and sea salt – it is important to have a set of precision kitchen scales with a resolution of at least 0.1 g. It is a worthwhile purchase. You also need a tablespoon and teaspoon for measuring.

What else is needed?
   A thermometer for checking the temperature of frying oil and water.
   A good knife with a sharpener, and if it's a Japanese knife, a whetstone.
   You can also buy a clay cooking pot, either a Japanese donabe or Chinese-style one (you can find one at an Oriental or Asian shop), as described in the section on cooking rice.

Then you can start to cook.
   When I write that Japanese cuisine is a simple cuisine, what that means for you, readers, is that no complicated processes or techniques await you. It's quick and easy most of the time.
   However, it might be a challenge when it comes to measuring with scales, teaspoons and tablespoons. You can also put aside the thought that everything will taste the same if there's soy sauce in it, which is what I actually thought about Japanese cuisine at first.
   Ultimately, the measures are more of a guide than a precise specification to be followed, given that every celery tastes different and every cook works in a different way; in the end, it all depends on your taste and the situation, the season and your guests. It's all about the coherence and culinary sense of the dishes, and that can mean using a gram here or a teaspoon there. And – never forget – it's all about the satisfaction you get from your own work.

ARRANGING

The potter and gastronome Kitaoji Rosanjin (1883–1959) once said that 'the vessel is clothing for the food inside'. Like dashi, the plate is the stage on which the vegetables can be showcased. There is a connection between the colours and shapes of vegetables and the crockery used. There are teachings and books that convey this relationship. Among other things, a distinction is made between a formal and a more informal arrangement. Round things go on rectangular dishes. The hassun is very special. Meaning 'eight *sun*', it's a platter that measures eight *sun* by eight *sun* (1 *sun* is equivalent to about 3 cm, so

about 24 x 24 cm) and plays an integral part in the serving of food in the tea ceremony, although it is now also a part of the courses served at fine Kaiseki restaurants. It is used to express a play on emptiness, which is actually as important in Zen Buddhism as being. Two foods are typically presented on the hassun, usually from the mountains and from the sea. They are presented in small piles, always one more than the number of diners. This was our inspiration for the spring dish 'Asparagus, black sesame and cherries' (page 40) and the autumn dish 'Grapes and walnuts' (page 123).

With the help of crockery, a tension is also built up between elements. Something that is not visible at first sight should be made to come alive, such as the actual taste of spring or autumn.

If a dish is made of unglazed ceramic, for example, it creates a direct connection with the earth. The crockery used for Japanese cuisine also changes with the seasons, even every month in certain top restaurants. In summer, it is supposed to convey coolness and therefore it is often made of glass and is moistened with water. In autumn, soup is often served in lacquer bowls covered with matching lids, with a golden or red leaf on the inside – an additional reference to the season. In winter, you can find a lot of earthenware, which retains heat well.

You need an awful lot of crockery to 'clothe' vegetables so exquisitely over and over again throughout the year. When it came to choosing crockery, we were guided by our motto of 'be satisfied with what is available and work with it', so we went and asked certain ceramists if we could arrange our dishes on their creations and take pictures of them. We were given a lot of help (the names of the ceramists are mentioned on page 204). We also had a few bowls and plates of our own.

Although there is a very extensive set of rules for the use of crockery in Japanese cuisine, we were guided by our intuition. We were also happy to be able to use a bowl or plate time and time again. After all, the value of things ultimately shows in their daily use. And even though Japanese ceramics are very expensive, they're really meant to be used for eating and drinking.

WHAT GOES WITH WHAT?

Cooking with the seasons is not an end in itself. The vegetables that are available in each season are at their peak, or, to put it more philosophically, have their essence at their most beautiful. Then all you really have to do is cut them, or showcase them using dashi and other means of adding umami flavour.

Here, the notion 'let us act in accordance with its nature' again comes to mind because nature doesn't always do what we want. On the contrary, we find, particularly against the background of monoculture and industrialised agriculture, that complete control and management of natural processes doesn't lead to the desired results. Ultimately, nature is a force we cannot control. In the context of our own surroundings, why in a year's time will the apple and quince trees be full of fruit but there will only be a scattering of plums? Why do the starlings strip this particularly cherry tree bare and what do I do about it? Why is the pumpkin plant spreading like a monster this summer? Understanding that there's something uncontrollable, which we like to call nature, leads to humility and gratitude.

Let's take things as they are – this is an attitude that the perfectionist in us initially tries to fight against. This was the case with us in the conceptual phase, when we were looking for the right way to do things. Whenever we would literally come to a dead end, this sentence allowed us to take a step back, laugh and start again with a smile on our face, or take a different path.

This is an exercise of which there are many in Zen Buddhism. It feels quite good to surpass yourself by lowering your expectations and letting yourself be guided by things. When you allow yourself to get involved with the vegetables, the moment, the place and the season, the togetherness and the circumstances, then everything comes together by itself.

The here and now is the time for all things. It means that asparagus can be paired with cherries, and quinces are a match for Brussels sprouts. What connects them is that they are available at the same time. Then you don't need cream, cheese, sauce or similar homogenising ingredients that we are used to in our local cuisine. This makes things pure and leads us to the essence of vegetables. And cooking will be easy. It's all about coming into contact with things, working with their qualities, accepting them. This can be a huge burden off your shoulders and a liberation. Think about the big meal you're planning and the pressure you feel when you imagine how your guests might judge you for any mistakes you make or because not everything is perfect. Here's where a carrot or celery can help you. They are what they are. Each already has its particular flavour; and besides, even if it doesn't turn out perfectly, who really cares? The alternative is much more difficult: messing things up completely.

So here's one last piece of advice: Let the vegetables guide you, and accept satisfaction when it comes.

When you focus your attention on cooking, the food you prepare will show that you have been attentive and kind, and that you have thought about the welfare of the vegetables, your guests and yourself.

People in Japan don't praise themselves or put themselves in the spotlight. Their dishes tell the story of who prepared and served them. And their guests eat and savour the carrot, capturing in it the taste of a host and cook who knows how to add flavour to things and to cook with the seasons.

That is our philosophy.

ABOUT QUANTITIES

The quantities given are intended to make several small dishes, as is common in Japan and much of Asia. In Japan, a basic meal typically consists of soup, rice and pickled vegetables or a side dish. Examples of this can be found at the end of the chapter on each season.

You are welcome to increase the quantities, for instance, when you need to make four portions. We feel that the portions are just large enough so that you can experience the vegetables without making you lose interest in them.

In Western cultures, people are often concerned about not feeling sated after a meal. If possible, just let the feeling pass and focus your awareness onto the meal you have just eaten that is inside you. Aren't there more positive things to compensate for not having a full belly? Like warmth, energy, an alert mind and the feeling of having done something good for yourself? We believe this is somewhat related to health. It's about taking good care of yourself and of others on different levels. It's equally about satisfaction – and perhaps even happiness, which we are so eager to pursue.

SPRING

◇◇◇

What exactly is spring?

The first thing that comes to mind is strawberries and asparagus, and then the moisture-laden and flower-scented wind in May, and we get the impression that spring is pure abundance. But impressions can be deceptive. Spring is also the changeability of April, the dreariness and cold of March, and the first heat of June.

Every year is different, and spring isn't a constant thing. For instance, the cold weather stayed with us until quite late in 2017, while the first heat of 2018 could already be felt in May.

As a result, it can sometimes take a longer or shorter time to have fresh vegetables from the garden and from the fields. We mainly pick herbs, shoots and stem and leaf vegetables. It's already summer by the time fruiting vegetables and fruits, such as aubergines and apricots, are ripe, while tubers and root vegetables often only emerge from the ground in autumn.

Until then, we have to make do with the vegetables and fruit stored from the last harvest. It pays to set aside provisions. All idyllic notions aside, however, at this time of year we are also dependent on imports from Italy, Spain and Egypt, and even Argentina and South Africa.

So what is spring? For us it's many things at once: clear and pure, earthy and airy, fragrant and sparse. It's awakening and dying quickly – just think of the short-lived cherry blossoms in Japan. It is protection in the soil, the force of shoots and sprouts, the soft white, bright green, the myriad colours of the flowers: elderflower, roses, dandelions and mallows. The potential of the world emerges and begins to unfold. Spring is transition and, not by chance as in the Christian faith, resurrection. It's a celebration and a true coming-into-being.

CARAMELISED
EDAMAME BEANS

Edamame beans make a wonderful snack. In Japan, these small green soya beans are popular nibbles to have with sake and beer. In an izakaya, the Japanese version of a pub, they're eaten straight from the pod.

We have drawn from this idea, but we feel edamame beans deserve to be turned into a dish of their own. And this is how we begin our spring menu. Sugar and sake accentuate their sweetness and soy sauce adds saltiness. Sugar and soy sauce are always a good combination, especially for grilled or fried food.

Serves 2

½ tsp sugar

4–5 tbsp edamame beans, shelled (can be frozen)

1 tsp sake

1 tsp light or dark soy sauce

Sprinkle the sugar into a small pan and gently shake and rotate the pan to distribute evenly. Heat until a caramel forms. It can turn a little dark. Add the beans and deglaze with the sake. Wait for a minute or so before adding the soy sauce. Gently shake and rotate the pan again. They're ready.

CLEAR SPRING SOUP

There is a wisdom to be found in this soup: simple things in particular require a lot of attention. The list of ingredients seems long, but it actually isn't; it just organises the ingredients in detail. The soup consists of kombu dashi, carrot, parsnip and wakame seaweed, plus the usual flavourings and flavour enhancers. It's a clear soup, which means you'll need to have gourmet sensitivity in order to make it appear empty and give it a full flavour at the same time, a fine tongue is required.

Traditionally, there are only two types of soup in Japan: miso soup, which is about the creaminess and depth of flavour of the miso, and clear soup. Here, the liquid becomes a setting for the things it contains. There are recipes that require the garnish to be cooked directly in the broth. In this case, however, the effect will be more delicate if each vegetable and the broth is given its own flavour.

Therefore, the quantities of sake, mirin, salt and sugar are only approximate. It's important, on the one hand, to feel your way slowly; and, on the other, to experiment with the different flavours. Although ingredients are added to the dashi, it has to give the impression that it hasn't actually been seasoned. The Western mindset is more accustomed to adding more, but this would quickly spoil its delicate nature. Depth, however, comes from having less. Because, as is well known, less is often more. Give it a try!

CLEAR SPRING SOUP

◇◇◇

This is the taste of early spring: the flavours of stored root vegetables, of the smooth, cool sea and of warming ginger, enveloped in the fullness of nothingness.

Serves 2

2 tsp dried wakame
    seaweed
500 ml kombu dashi
2–4 tsp sake
2–4 tsp mirin
1 tsp light soy sauce
½–1 tsp salt
2–3 pinches sugar

1 medium carrot
2 tbsp kombu dashi
1 tsp sake
1 tsp mirin
1 pinch salt
1 pinch sugar

1 medium parsnip
2 tbsp kombu dashi
1 tbsp sake
1 pinch salt
1 pinch sugar

1 tsp fresh ginger
1 tsp sake
½ tsp sugar

Soften the dried seaweed in cold water.

Heat the kombu dashi. First, add the sake and mirin to the dashi and taste. Next, add the soy sauce and taste. Then add a little salt and taste. Then add some sugar. What was previously a rather thin broth suddenly becomes denser, fuller-bodied and sweeter. Ideally, the taste of the salt should be unnoticeable, yet the soup shouldn't taste unsalted.

Peel and cut up the carrot. Combine with the kombu dashi, sake and mirin. Cover with a lid and cook over a medium heat until the centre of the carrot is still slightly crunchy. Ideally, the liquid should boil away completely. Otherwise, transfer the carrot to a plate to cool, reduce the cooking liquid and mix with the carrot. Taste a little and season with very little salt and sugar until the flavour is balanced.

Repeat the process with the parsnip: peel, cut, add kombu dashi and sake, and cook. Remove the parsnip, reduce the liquid and mix. Then season with a few grains of salt and sugar.

Peel and slice the ginger, and then cut it into very thin julienne strips. Mix with sake and sugar, bring to the boil and remove from the heat. Drain the seaweed and gently squeeze.

It's time to layer the ingredients in a soup bowl. Arrange the seaweed at the bottom of the bowl with the carrot, parsnip and ginger over it. Then pour over the hot broth and serve.

SILKEN TOFU, RAINBOW CHARD AND MANDARIN DRESSING

Rainbow chard is one of the most beautiful spring vegetables, and for us it's the symbol of spring: It shoots upwards with great vitality, forming flexible stems and large leaves, but its colour and flavour are still delicate.

Cooking is cutting. Chard is a good example of this. 'Since we've been cutting it into batons like the ones in this recipe, my family suddenly likes it very much,' Jule told me a few days after we had cooked and photographed the dish.

And it was the same for me. The green, thick Swiss chard that was once served in school canteens – coarsely cut across the stalk and then cooked until grey and soft – was an example of how things could be debased or buried under a layer of thick white sauce. But we do things very differently.

We very lightly blanch the chard, Japanese style, which consists of holding it in boiling water. This keeps it crisp and a little firm, which contrasts nicely with the soft and creamy tofu. The special touch comes from the dressing made with real mandarin. It tingles nicely on the tongue and embodies the spirit of spring, being both sweet and savoury at the same time. Incidentally, in Japan you would use mikan, a citrus fruit that is closely related to the satsuma.

The tricky part comes with the tofu that is available to us. Organic tofu, especially silken tofu, is often too bitter or tart, and somehow quite dreary. You should therefore use varieties available at Oriental or Asian shops.

Serves 2

Salt

3–4 medium stalks (about 100 g) rainbow chard

1 tbsp sesame oil

100 g silken tofu

For the dressing

4 tsp organic mandarin marmalade

1 tsp light soy sauce

2 tsp lemon juice

2 tsp kombu dashi or water

For the chard, bring salted water to the boil in a pan. Fill a bowl with cold water. Hold the chard by the leaves and dip the stems into the boiling water for 20–30 seconds. Refresh briefly in cold water. Now turn the chard upside down, and holding it by the stems, dip the leaves in the boiling water for 10 seconds. Refresh in cold water and leave to drain. Separate the leaves from the stems. Cut the stems into finger-length batons the thickness of a pencil, and cut the leaves lengthways into strips roughly the width of a finger. Mix stems and leaves separately with the sesame oil and 1 pinch of salt.

For the dressing, mix the mandarin marmalade with the light soy sauce, lemon juice and kombu dashi.

Cut the tofu into four pieces and cover with the dressing. Arrange with the chard and serve.

SPRING VEGETABLE TEMPURA

⬦⬦⬦

The leaf-to-root movement has a special role for carrot tops. They smell very aromatic and appetising, but they're somewhat woody and tough. As tempura, however, their fine taste is captured, while making them pleasantly crunchy to chew. The batter should be thin so that it doesn't form thick clumps between the frond-like leaves. Large tops aren't easy to dip in the dipping sauce and eat, but that makes it all the more fun. In addition, you also eat the whole carrot and whole radish, and savour the delicate and resinous tartness of the young celery. Instead of the typical flakes of smoked bonito, known as katsuobushi, we use a combination of kombu kelp, dried tomato and shiitake mushroom for the dipping sauce.

Serves 2

2 baby carrots with tops
4 radishes
2 small sticks celery with
    leaves (from the centre
    of the head)
3–4 tbsp plain flour, for
    dusting
90 g plain flour
Oil, for deep-frying

For the dipping sauce

2 g kombu kelp
2 small (about 1 g) dried
    shiitake mushrooms
1 (4–5 g) dried tomato
13 ml mirin
1 tsp sake
13 ml light soy sauce
½–1 tsp sugar

For the dipping sauce, heat 70 ml of water to about 60°C/140°F. Add the kombu, mushrooms and dried tomato and steep for 30 minutes. Remove the kombu, mushrooms and tomato. Heat the liquid, add the mirin, sake and soy sauce, and bring to the boil. Then remove from the heat and leave to cool. Adjust the flavour with sugar.

For the tempura, heat the oil to 180°C/356°F. Place the vegetables on the work surface and dust with flour. Turn over and dust again.

For the batter, sift the 90 g flour into a bowl. Make an ice bath by lining a large bowl with ice packs (preferably gel-filled) and filling with water. Place a smaller bowl inside to make the batter. Put 140 ml of ice-cold water into the small bowl. Add the flour and mix loosely and quickly with a set of chopsticks. There should be lumps in the batter. The batter should stick to the vegetables in a light and thin layer.

One by one, dip the flour-dusted vegetables in the batter, immerse in the hot oil and deep-fry until the bubbles become small and the hissing sound dies down. Lift out with a skimmer and leave to drain. NB: Deep-fry the tempura in small batches. Do not put too many vegetables into the oil at the same time. The temperature should never fall below 170°C/338°F or the batter will turn mushy.

Serve immediately, dip in the dipping sauce and eat up every little bit.

By the way, carrot tops require a little more skill. Our advice is to slide the carrot into the oil first, then slowly let the top slip into the oil after it in an arc along the side of the pan. It's well worth the effort. This is one of our favourite dishes!

Tip: Give the dipping sauce a nice twist with grated zest of an untreated lemon or lime and a splash or two of the juice.

BEANS, RADISHES AND DILL

—◇◇◇—

The inspiration for this dish came to us in an unusual way. We were in the kitchen and had this idea to do something with beans that would highlight their smooth and coolness, while having something fresh and substantial at the same time. It takes some time before the first local spring produce becomes available. They typically start with the smaller and delicate things, like herbs and radishes.

Somehow things came together, and radishes ended up being sliced and added to our lightly sour bean salad.

The third element, dill, is a mostly overlooked herb that tends to be used only to a very limited extent. So that it can be appreciated, and because it develops a special flavour in large amounts, this dish contains a generous serving of dill.

Serves 2

50 g dried beans (e.g. haricot or flageolet beans)

2 tbsp kombu dashi

2 tbsp rice vinegar

1 tsp sugar

2–3 pinches salt

4 radishes

2 medium-sized fresh dill fronds or 3 tbsp leaves, coarsely plucked

Soak the beans according to the instructions on the package and cook until soft in plenty of water. Drain and marinate in a mixture of kombu dashi, rice vinegar, sugar and salt for about 10 minutes. The marinade will be absorbed into the beans, so they will have to be seasoned again with salt, sugar and possibly vinegar. The longer the beans are allowed to marinate, the more consistent their flavour will be. They can also be prepared the day before.

Slice the radishes. Mix together with the dill and beans. Chilled, this salad is also great for the first warm days of the year.

MISO POTATOES AND CELERY

◇◇◇

Celery makes a wonderful combination with the first potatoes of the year, which are firm and almost crunchy but still have a light flavour. Celery is minerally and juicy, and the young leaves are wonderfully resinous and bitter, and every bite is a discovery, like walking a fine line, of whether this bitterness is pleasant or not.

The bitter flavour of the leaves can be toned down if they are prepared as tempura together with their stalks (see Spring vegetable tempura, page 35), which also allows a use to be given to the parts of the celery that would otherwise end up in the compost heap.

Stewing potatoes and celery in miso gives them a delicate creaminess. Shiitake mushroom subtly boosts the flavour and brings this dish closer to a traditional potato salad, especially when garnished with chives. While the dish tastes familiar, it's Japanese inspiration still keeps it unique.

Serves 3–4
200 ml kombu dashi
½ dried shiitake
*   mushroom*
250 g potatoes
2 tbsp white miso paste
2 sticks celery
1–2 chive or garlic chive
*   leaves (with flowers)*

Lightly warm the dashi in a pan and steep the mushroom in the liquid for 15 minutes.

Peel and halve the potatoes and cut into wedges. Remove the mushroom from the dashi and add the potatoes. Bring to the boil and simmer gently for 10 minutes. Add the miso paste and cook for 2–3 more minutes. The potatoes should still be a little firm. It is best to check from time to time. Ideally, the sauce should be thick and creamy. If not, take out the potatoes and reduce the sauce.

Slice the celery on a diagonal. Blanch to taste. If it's too raw and chewy, it will overpower the dish. If left too long, it will become soft and limp and lose its resinous aroma. Blanching for 2 minutes is recommended. Then refresh in cold water.

Finely chop the chives. Mix the miso potatoes with the celery and garnish with chives. This dish tastes better served lukewarm or cold.

ASPARAGUS, BLACK SESAME AND CHERRIES

Sometimes things happen by chance. In fact, they literally come to you. Just like the time we were thinking about working with asparagus and the first birds were attacking the cherries that hung ripe and bright on the tree. A fruit and a vegetable on the same plate; would that work? Yes, we believed it could. The connection between the fruit and the vegetable was made using notes of black sesame and lemon. The cherries are lightly flavoured with sake and soy sauce to bring them into the realm of 'savoury'. Asparagus and cherries meet in the middle of the plate, where there is nothing.

The dish draws on the notion of the hassun course of Kaiseki cuisine, particularly accompanying the tea ceremony (see page 18-19). Things from the mountains and things from the sea are arranged very formally in small piles with straight edges and set diagonally to each other; and there are always as many piles as there are guests attending the tea ceremony, plus one more so that no one has to take the last piece on the tray.

Our concept is somewhat different. It is designed to serve two people, and it mainly highlights the contrasts between colours, shapes and fruit and vegetable while creating harmony. The untainted natural green of the asparagus meets the smooth, deep red of the cherries.

Serves 2

150 g green asparagus
    spears
2 tbsp black sesame seeds
1 tsp mirin
Sake
Soy sauce
Sugar
1 dash lemon juice
Grated zest of 1 untreated
    lemon
1 pinch of salt (optional)
100 g sweet cherries

Peel the asparagus only as much as is necessary; usually just the lower third is sufficient. It's best to just try it. Cut off the woody ends. Steam the spears for 2 minutes and refresh in a bowl with plenty of cold water.

Toast the sesame seeds in a frying pan over a low heat and coarsely crush in a mortar. Combine the mirin with a teaspoon of sake, a dash of soy sauce, 2 tablespoons of sugar, lemon juice and the grated zest in a saucepan and bring to the boil, then remove from the heat and mix in the sesame seeds. Add the asparagus and turn to coat well. Adjust the seasoning with salt if necessary. Arrange on a plate.

Pit the cherries. Put a pinch of sugar into a saucepan and cook to a light caramel. Add the cherries and shake and rotate the saucepan once. Add a dash of sake and half a teaspoon of soy sauce. Shake and rotate the pan again. Then arrange the cherries on the plate. The cherries should be lightly glazed with the sauce but still raw.

GRILLED KING OYSTER MUSHROOMS AND SPRING ONIONS

————◇◇◇————

Light and zesty spring onions and thick, crumbly mushrooms make a simple and beautiful combination. We put both on the barbecue together with tofu dengaku, miso-glazed tofu (see following recipe, page 46). Then we completed our lovely dinner by the fire with a bowl of rice and some pickled vegetables.

There's an almost infinite number of possible variations using the basic ingredients of the marinade. The essential element is the combination of soy sauce and sweetness, which produces the wonderful smell that pervades a lot of izakaya and simple restaurants in Japan.

After halving the spring onions, we only grill the rounded outer surface of the bulbs. That way they stay juicy. The mouth-watering moment comes when the heat of the embers makes the onion juices start to bubble on the cut surface and caramelise at the edges.

The recipe is quick and easy to make. Naturally, you can also use other sorts of mushrooms, but the king oyster mushrooms are particularly good because they're thick and fleshy.

GRILLED KING OYSTER MUSHROOMS AND SPRING ONIONS

$\diamond\!\diamond\!\diamond$

Serves 2

*2 spring onions (with the
most developed bulbs
possible)*
2 king oyster mushrooms

For the marinade

20 ml sake
30 ml mirin
30 ml soy sauce
*1–2 pinches of salt,
according to preference*

Combine the ingredients for the marinade and bring to the boil, flambéing if necessary to burn off the alcohol. Then leave to cool. Cut the spring onions and mushrooms in half lengthways and marinate for at least half an hour. I like to use a resealable plastic bag for this. Pressing the air out is sort of like vacuum sealing the bag, and this works well with small amounts of marinade.

Remove the mushrooms and spring onions from the marinade and drain lightly on a plate. Heat up a barbecue or a Japanese-style grill (see page 72). If you decide to use a Japanese grill, proceed as follows: thread a skewer through the bottom of the mushroom halves (use skewers that are as long and thin as possible). Then thread another skewer through the top of the mushrooms (just below the cap) with a second roasting spit. You will end up with two skewers in your hand with the mushrooms threaded on side by side.

It's best to use three skewers for the spring onions. Thread a skewer through the bulbs, another through the light green middle section and the last through the top of the leaves (you can fold over any excess).

Place the skewers with the mushrooms and spring onions over the grill until the mushrooms and onions are golden brown and caramelised. Grill the mushrooms on both sides, but the spring onions only need to be grilled with the cut side facing upwards. You can also experiment with the spring onion leaves if you thread the skewers closer together, letting parts of the leaves hang down between them, closer to the embers. This will result in more colour and develop their flavours.

Remove both vegetables from the grill and serve.

TOFU DENGAKU

———◇◇◇———

Dengaku is the Japanese name for a sauce made of miso and a few seasoning ingredients that is spread as a glaze on vegetables and tofu, as here, after grilling. These make exquisite and substantial dishes, especially in the vegan Shojin Ryori of Zen temples and monasteries. Incidentally, aubergine is considered a meat substitute in Japan. While tofu has long been known to us for the same reason. Both tofu dengaku and aubergine dengaku, are highly nutritious dishes on their own. The miso sauce is slightly sweet and goes very well with the main ingredient chosen. Light and dark miso sauce are very common.

Serves 2
150 g firm tofu

For the dengaku sauce
100 g red (aka) miso paste (for a milder-flavoured sauce replace a quarter of the amount with white miso paste)
2 tbsp sake
2 tbsp mirin
2 tbsp sugar
6 tbsp kombu dashi

Combine the miso paste, sake, mirin, sugar and dashi in a pan and bring to the boil and allow to thicken to the original consistency of the miso paste. Stir constantly.

Cut the tofu into rectangles (about the size of a chocolate bar). Japanese recipes tell you to squeeze it well and then to grill it lightly golden on both sides, before spreading it with the sauce and grilling again, but it isn't necessary.

We prefer the tofu to be moist, so it is enough to pat both sides dry with kitchen paper and spread the sauce thickly on one side (the flavour will soak through the tofu). Then thread two metal skewers at the short ends of each tofu piece and grill it on both sides until it is brown on the bottom and slightly caramelised on the glazed side.

It tastes good very hot, but it can also be served cold.

SANGOHACHI-MARINATED YOUNG SPINACH AND SEARED SHIMEJI MUSHROOMS

———◇◇◇———

This dish has an essentially nutty flavour, although this is hardly suggested by spinach and mushroom. However, they combine with the marinade to create this beautiful flavour. We blanched and marinated the spinach in the Japanese style, and in doing so we realised that it was practically like taking a leaf-to-root approach because it makes use of the bright pink root crown and its beauty is also often showcased. Together with the stalks and leaves, the three essential and yet very different parts of the spinach are eaten.

Somewhat unusually for us, the mushrooms are first seared in a frying pan, or you can do this on a barbecue if you like, and then marinated in the same paste as the spinach so they soak it up completely. They give the dish a soft and creamy texture and bring out the nuttiness.

This flavour is enhanced invisibly but no less effectively by the marinade. Sangohachi is a thin, lightly salted paste made from rice fermented using koji mould, a type of fungus. It has a clean fermented flavour with added sweetness and saltiness. But the special part is the clear liquid in between the rice grains, which acts like an umami lacquer. It enhances the flavour of the thick, neat spinach and the crunchy, creamy mushrooms, creating out of both a beautiful oneness and harmony that is mellow and satisfying, and at the same time a little strange and quietly exotic.

SANGOHACHI-MARINATED YOUNG SPINACH AND SEARED SHIMEJI MUSHROOMS

◇◇◇

Serves 2

200 g young spinach
  with leaves as tender
  as possible (preferably
  whole heads, including
  the root and leaves)
Salt
Oil for the pan
About 100 g shimeji
  mushrooms (also
  known as white beech
  mushrooms, available
  from Asian or Oriental
  shops), alternatively
  enoki mushrooms

For the marinade

90 ml kombu dashi
10 g sangohachi (see page
  49), alternatively 1 tsp
  white miso paste
1 tbsp mirin
1 tbsp light soy sauce
1 pinch salt
1 pinch sugar

Combine the ingredients for the marinade in a saucepan, bring to the boil, and strain through a sieve. Set aside.

Remove any wilted leaves from the spinach. Cut off the root at the base of the crown. Bring salted water to the boil for blanching and prepare a bowl of cold water. Carefully hold the spinach by its leaves and dip the stems and root crown into the boiling salted water. Blanch for about 20 seconds and then briefly refresh in the cold water. Now hold the spinach by its base and stems and quickly dip the leaves into the boiling water. This should only take two seconds. Refresh again. Drain well and squeeze a little to remove the excess water. Put the whole heads in a deep dish or baking dish and gently massage in half the marinade. Set aside.

Use kitchen paper to oil the surface of a frying pan. Sear the mushrooms on both sides over high heat. This should take about 2 minutes each side, depending on the type of cooker and frying pan. Mix the mushrooms in a small bowl with the rest of the marinade and leave to stand for 1–2 minutes.

Drain the spinach a little and cut the root crown, stems and leaves into equal lengths. Arrange on a plate with the mushrooms. Add more of the marinade to taste.

Tip: The dish can be easily complemented with hazelnuts, the epitome of nuttiness.

TSUKEMONO
PICKLED SPRING VEGETABLES

—◇◇◇—

Tsukemono is the name given to preserved or pickled vegetables, which in Japan are often served with rice and soup at the end of the meal. These are made using a wide variety of different techniques and preparations. You can use practically any of the most common vegetables.

Here we show a simple variation that can be enjoyed after just an hour or two, although it tastes better after a day.

Radishes and turnips are often fermented whole, from the tip of the leaves to the roots. Likewise, we pickle the radishes and kohlrabi together with their leaves and stems. They lose some of their bitterness during the pickling process. They're cut into smaller pieces before serving. This makes them easier to eat and better to enjoy. Incidentally, cherry leaves add a unique aroma and taste.

Serves 2

½ or 1 small kohlrabi with
  leaves
½ bunch radishes
Salt
1 sheet (about 2 g) kombu
  kelp
1 strip zest from an
  untreated lemon
4 tbsp rice vinegar
2 tsp cane sugar
Cherry leaves

Cut the kohlrabi into vertical slices and put into a deep baking dish with the radishes. Sprinkle with salt, especially the leaves, and lightly rub in. Rest for 20 minutes and then rinse. This removes part of their bitterness.

I like to do the pickling in resealable bags. They're quite handy and fit in any corner of the fridge or kitchen cupboards. It's easy to squeeze out the air and only a little liquid is needed for pickling. Put the vegetables, kombu, lemon zest, vinegar, sugar and cherry leaves in a bag. Weigh the filled bag and add 2 per cent of its weight in salt. The salt and sugar ensure a brine forms. Roll up the bag, squeezing out the air, and weigh the bag down with a weight, such as a stone.

Leave to stand at room temperature, turning from time to time and removing any air again if necessary – this allows the brine to completely surround the vegetables – and replace the weight. The pickling process is faster in warm weather, but it slows down inside the fridge. This means that the intensity of the pickling can be determined by the maker.

Before serving, lightly squeeze the excess liquid from the kohlrabi and radish leaves. Finely slice the kohlrabi leaves and cut the kohlrabi into slices the thickness of a chopstick. The radishes are good to eat whole. These pickles are at their best after one day and served chilled on the first hot days of the year.

WHITE MISO SOUP WITH TOFU AND SPRING ONION

———◇◇◇———

There is a tender side to spring. The sun's rays only have a gentle warmth and the first green to emerge from the soil does so very timidly. The year is still relatively new and fresh.

This soup made of white miso paste with silken tofu is a good representation. The first signs of green are in the form of thin rings. However, there is a certain depth and intensity felt through the saltiness and ripeness of the miso.

Clear, simple and clean, this for us is the taste of the arrival of spring and what is to come.

Serves 2

80–100 g silken tofu

500 ml kombu dashi

45 g white miso paste

½ spring onion

Cut the tofu into cubes.

Heat the dashi. Put the miso into a sieve, hold the sieve in the dashi and use a spoon to press the miso through the sieve. This keeps any pieces of rice or soya beans from entering the broth. Add the tofu. Don't bring the soup to the boil, just keep it warm.

Cut the spring onion into thin rings. Divide the miso soup, tofu and spring onion into two bowls and serve.

Tip: Because the soup is so simple, it's advisable to use good-quality miso paste.

METHOD FOR COOKING RICE

—◇◇◇—

The Japanese way of cooking rice (and grains in general) is extraordinary. You'd think it was one of hardest things ever. Just the thought of it conjures up the image of a Japanese person looking sternly over your shoulder and you feel the only thing you're capable of is failure. Then you feel it's best not to even try.

But cooking rice is not as difficult as it might seem. If you overcome your fears and even dare to fail, things become easier. Cooking rice follows a certain rhythm that soon becomes second nature. It's also reassuring when you research the subject to discover just how many approaches to cooking rice and recipes there actually are.

It took us a while, but we finally found our preferred technique.

Ingredients for 2 portions — *140 g rice (round grain rice, e.g. organic pudding rice)*

WHAT TO DO

Put the rice in a tall container and cover it with plenty of water. Then gently swish the rice around with your hand. The water will become cloudy. Pour it out, refill the container with fresh water and repeat the process until the water runs mostly clear. This may mean having to do this five times and taking up to ten minutes. A Zen Buddhist would probably say that eighty per cent is enough.

Washing rice is also an exercise in mindfulness. This devotion to rice is still found in Japan today, and is present in cookbooks, private homes and professional kitchens. You can't cook rice just like that. It takes time and care.

The rice should rest after washing. Pour away the washing water and leave the rice to absorb the water adhering to the grains. I find that 30 minutes is enough time to rest rice. Some people recommend an hour. The rice will also be fine, however, if it's cooked immediately after washing.

HOW TO COOK

Weigh the rested, now swollen rice and add 110 per cent of its weight in water; i.e. for every 160 g of rested rice, add about 180 ml of water.

I acquired a donabe, a Japanese clay cooking pot, from a Japanese potter to use for this cookbook, and I've been cooking with it on gas and very enthusiastically ever since. It gives the rice a very different quality. It begins with the lovely smell that comes out of the small hole in the lid as it cooks and ends with the anticipation you feel before you open the lid and see the result for the first time. And rice steamed in a clay pot also has a lovely appearance. The whole process is actually a very aesthetic experience. This is probably due to the rhythm with which the rice cooks: you slowly bring it to temperature, you sustain it, and then you let it subside. There's something quite musical about it.

Of course, the recipe also works if you use a normal pan, preferably one with a glass lid so you can see what's happening inside. However, using a clay pot means it will be slower for you to react, so you have to have a clear idea of what to do.

Once you cover the rice with water, put the lid on the pan and place it over a medium heat. Every cooker is different, so whether you use a gas, electric or ceramic hob, you need to be very familiar with the way it works. When the water comes to the boil, reduce the heat to the lowest setting and continue to cook until the water is gone. You can tell from the sound the pan makes. There's a very subtle difference between the bubbling of the rice as it cooks and the crackling of the rice as it dries.

Take off the lid, wipe away any water from the rim of the pan, put the lid back on and leave the rice to rest for another 15 minutes. Then it's ready.

Rice swells, which means that it's more about time than it is about heat. In a nutshell: bring it to the boil slowly, let it evaporate slowly over a gentle heat and simply allow it to swell.

Then carefully fluff the finished rice with a wooden paddle or a rubber spatula. The Japanese also take great care when it comes to this, so that all the grains stay intact and don't get squashed. This allows them to show their fine lustre and round beauty. The rice should be light and fluffy and yet the grains should stick to each other firmly, which actually sounds like a contradiction.

If you're lucky, or well-practised, you'll find that a golden crust has formed on the bottom of the pot. The rice grains should have a delicate, sticky texture on the outside and be clear in the middle.

Other cereals can also be cooked using this method. In this book we make suggestions for buckwheat and barley (see pages 61 and 104). If you're feeling experimental, you can also try it out with other grains such as oats or spelt.

ABOUT THE TYPE OF RICE

Some of my Japanese friends who live in Europe use organic pudding rice from Italy. They miss using round Japanese rice, but the price and the long distance it has to come make it unsuitable for daily use. We've tried different varieties and have had satisfactory results with organic pudding rice.

Tip: A very nice and simple variation is rice with edamame beans. Before cooking, simply add 3–4 tablespoons of peeled edamame beans after weighing the rice.

GINGER RICE

White rice accompanied only with ginger, with its subtle colour, is a small but tasteful and elegant celebration of simplicity. If black rice is added, the dish is enhanced with a nutty taste, a slightly grainy and crispy texture and a hint of wildness. It reminds us of its botanical origins: rice is a grass.

The black rice colours the dish a delicate violet. The sake, soy sauce and a little salt are also added at the start. They give the rice its elegance. The choice to use only white rice or to mix it with black grains was not easy. Both options have their own beauty.

Serves 2

140 g white round rice (or 120 g white round rice mixed with 20 g black rice)

2 tsp sake

1 tsp light soy sauce

2 pinches salt

1 tsp ginger, cut into julienne strips

Mix both types of rice together (otherwise use only white rice) and wash thoroughly until the water is clear. Drain well and rest for 30 minutes. Weigh the rested rice, add the same amount of water plus 10 per cent and then add the sake, soy sauce and salt.

Cover the pan with a lid and bring to the boil over a medium heat. Reduce the heat to the lowest setting and continue cooking the rice until you hear it start to crackle. Take off the lid and wipe the rim of the pan, put the ginger on the rice and put the lid back on.

Remove the pan from the heat and leave the rice to rest for at least 15 minutes. Carefully fluff and mix the rice.

BUCKWHEAT

—◇◇◇—

We felt it was very important to show a variety of grains and cereals and how to cook with them. When they're prepared as cleanly as Japanese rice, they wonderfully reveal their essence.

Buckwheat also grows in the higher, cold regions of the world, where little else can be grown. It can be found in the cuisines of Russia, northern France and Japan. Buckwheat can be both warming and relieve the sensation of heat at the same time, which makes it perfect for spring and its changeable nature. Likewise, it can be eaten hot immediately after cooking or left to cool down.

It can be cooked using our favourite rice recipe. In this way you can experience buckwheat in all its beauty and rich flavour, grain by grain.

Serves 2

120 g buckwheat

Wash the buckwheat in a tall container with plenty of water, changing the water repeatedly until it runs clear. This process doesn't take as long as washing rice. Pour away the water. Leave to rest and swell for 30 minutes.

Weigh the rested buckwheat and add 110 per cent of its weight in water.

Put the buckwheat and water into a pan (preferably with a glass lid). We also use the donabe pot for this.

Bring to the boil over a medium heat. Reduce the heat to the lowest setting and cook the buckwheat until the water boils away and you hear a light crackling sound. Take off the lid, wipe away any water from the rim of the pan, put the lid back on and leave the buckwheat to rest near the stove for another 15 minutes.

Carefully fluff the buckwheat as with the steamed white rice and serve hot or cold.

STRAWBERRIES AND RHUBARB IN ELDERFLOWER JELLY

There are no desserts in the Western sense in traditional Japanese cuisine. Delicate wagashi, sweets made from beans and sugar are served during the tea ceremony; otherwise, there's fruit.

Fruits in jelly may be a tribute to French cuisine, which is highly appreciated by a number of leading Japanese chefs. Unfortunately, not much importance is given to jelly in this country, and we think it's a shame. It has a wonderfully cooling effect, not only because it's served cold, but because it has a smooth consistency and its gloss is pleasing to the eye. In short: we need more jelly.

We took fruits that are available locally in May – strawberries and rhubarb – and flavoured the jelly with whole-cane sugar. This type of sugar is highly prized, where it's used, for instance, to make wagashi and kuromitsu, a rich and dark sugar syrup which was the inspiration for this jelly.

East meets West in a serene moment with a cooling jelly, which can easily be accompanied by a bowl of matcha. If you want to give this dessert a more Western feel, serve it together with zabaglione.

Serves 2

100 g rhubarb
200 g strawberries
1 pinch salt
2 g agar-agar
20 g demerara sugar
1–2 tsp whole-cane sugar
1 strip zest from an
    untreated lemon
1 elderflower head

Cut the rhubarb into 3–4-cm lengths, steam for 2–3 minutes and leave to cool. The pieces should still be a little firm and crunchy. Clean the strawberries.

Combine 150 ml water with the salt and agar-agar and mix well to dissolve. Put both types of sugar into a small saucepan and caramelise. Add the dissolved agar-agar and cook until the mixture thickens. Remove from the heat and add the lemon zest. Leave to cool until lukewarm. Cut off each of the elderberry flowers at the base of the stem and add to the jelly mixture. Remove the zest.

Make layers of strawberries and rhubarb in a small, deep bowl and pour the elderflower-infused jelly over the top. Refrigerate for at least 1 hour.

The jelly stays very soft and is unsuitable for moulding. Instead, it envelops the fruit and melts easily in the mouth.

ANKO WITH LEMON

If you pare down traditional Japanese sweets to the essentials, you'll find that they consist of two basic ingredients: beans, red azuki beans (also known as aduki and adzuki beans) to be precise, and sugar. The paste made from them is known as an or anko. It comes in two basic forms: koshian is a smooth paste that has been sieved, while tsubushian is a coarser paste made by mashing the beans. However, we had a different idea, namely to leave the beans for this recipe as whole as possible and to candy them. The skins remain a little tough because of this, so you have to chew well. Anko tastes best fresh in any form, and the pinch of salt added at the end adds a particular kick to the whole dish.

Our personal favourite is anko with lots of lemon. The generous addition of finely sliced lemon zest takes the dessert out of the typical range of Japanese flavours and makes it something unique and very harmonious.

Serves 4

100 g azuki beans
80–90 g sugar
1 pinch salt
½ untreated lemon

Cover the beans with plenty of water and bring to the boil (top up the water as they cook if too much evaporates). Cook over a medium heat, covered with a lid, until soft (until you can easily crush the beans between your fingers). Drain the beans and return them to the pan. Add the sugar and salt, bring to the boil and cook until the sugar dissolves. Stir gently.

Peel off the zest and then squeeze the lemon. Cut the zest into very thin julienne strips. Carefully mix the juice and zest into the bean. They should be enveloped in a creamy and glossy liquid.

Serve while still warm. This dish goes well with matcha – a classic combination reminiscent of a tea ceremony.

Tip: It isn't worth your while to cook only a small amount; on the contrary, a large portion can be easily be eaten or frozen.

You can experiment with different types of sugar. Using refined sugar, raw sugar or whole-cane sugar greatly varies the flavour, as does the amount of sugar you add to the beans. Traditional Japanese recipes use a ratio of one part sugar to one part beans.

MATCHA

According to many Japanese cooks, it all begins with the water. They can't cook without the right kind of water. The same goes for making Japanese tea. The water should be soft and not impose. It should allow the full flavour of the green tea to develop. You can use filtered water, good spring water or tap water in places with soft water.

Not all matcha is the same either. Because the whole leaf is used and drunk, we wanted to use tea grown organically, without the use of synthetic fertilisers and pesticides. This tea has less umami than conventionally grown tea, but then drinking it becomes enjoyable on various levels because health and pleasure are considered equally.

Matcha produces a special alertness. Like coffee, it is quickly absorbed by the body, but it has a long-lasting effect similar to that of other green teas.

It comes as no surprise that it is drunk in Zen monasteries as it helps concentration to be focused on the essentials, meditation and daily practice on the path to enlightenment.

Matcha is the highlight of the traditional tea ceremony. And if food is served, it is eaten first, before the tea is offered to end the ceremony. We do things the same way, always leaving the tea for the end of our seasonal selection of dishes.

Makes 1 serving

2 g matcha (of a high quality grade, preferably organic)

Soak the tines of the chasen (bamboo matcha whisk) to soften.

Bring water to the boil. Pour 80 ml of boiling water into the bowl to be used to drink the tea. Then pour the same water into another bowl. Every time water is poured into a different bowl, its temperature drops by 10°C. The temperature of the water should be 80°C at most. Under this temperature, everything is possible, even matcha served with ice, although this variation has a different taste.

Sieve the matcha powder directly into the drinking bowl. Add the water. Whisk the tea with the chasen, starting at the bottom of the bowl and loosely moving in the shape of an 'M' using your wrist. Then slowly lift the chasen to the surface while whisking. The foam forming should be as fine as possible.

Enjoy your matcha with anko, Japanese sweets or a dried fruit, which should be eaten before.

SUMMER

Summer is the season we would always look forward to as a child. Although in the last few years it seems to be getting hotter and hotter; at least that's how we feel. And with it, the need to escape the heat and cool down increases. In Japan, particularly in Kyoto, summer is the busiest season: Temperatures there hover around 30 degrees. Added to this is the humidity, which some say even turns salt liquid. And this sultriness is everywhere, unless you turn on the air conditioning, which removes the humidity together with the heat.

Relief also comes in the shape of food. In Japan, relief from the heat comes in many different ways. Serving dishes are often made of polished glass, dishes are served cold, and vegetables such as aubergines are particularly popular. They soak up cold broth like a sponge and release it into your mouth when you bite into them. Even the slightest hint of coolness – the glistening on the surface of water, the presentiment of the first winds of late summer and even a refreshing thought – are gratefully received. This also makes the subject of refreshment and cooling important for us.

But aside from this, what else does summer actually mean? There is a sharper contrast between light and shade, between heat and coolness (and if that's not enough, it helps to jump into water or to have ice cream). And as the season settles in, things settle down. Waiting for late summer and harvest time or the first tomatoes, berries and other summer fruits for us is as much a part of the season as being outdoors, which we all enjoy. Summer is a social time. And it's a busy, exciting and colourful time.

GREEN BEANS WITH WHITE SESAME SEEDS

———◇◇◇———

Outside in the garden the French beans are growing. At what for plants is a breathtaking pace, they seek the light, and their tips have already reached the end of the long poles put up to support them. Above them there is only the sky, which is almost continuously clear and blue at this time.

The beans seem to be filled with a good deal of energy, which comes through when they are only briefly steamed and refreshed, and served firm to the bite.

We serve them coated in a sauce made with sangohachi, a paste made from rice fermented with koji mould and salt. Pure umami. We combine it with toasted sesame seeds to help stick to the beans. We find that they enhance the flavour.

Serves 2

100 g French beans
3 tbsp white sesame seeds
1 tsp sangohachi,
*   alternatively 2 tsp*
*   white miso paste*
2 tbsp kombu dashi
½ tsp sugar
1 tsp mirin

Steam the beans for 4–5 minutes, depending on their thickness, and refresh in a bowl of cold water. Drain on a cloth. Depending on their flavour and size, cut them in half or into thirds along their length.

Dry-roast the sesame seeds in a frying pan over a medium heat and coarsely crush in a mortar. Combine the remaining ingredients, bring to the boil and strain through a fine-mesh sieve. Mix the sesame seeds with the marinade and taste it: is there anything missing? Does it need saltiness or sweetness? Then add the beans to the sauce, coat well and serve.

METHOD FOR GRILLING

The art of grilling as practised in Japan is quite different from the way it is done in the West. In some professional kitchens you can now see a long rectangular box-like container filled with glowing Japanese charcoal with skewers of food sizzling over it. Binchotan is the name given to a special charcoal that gives off practically no smoke. It can be used for grilling indoors without the thick smoke produced by a conventional barbecue. But the beauty of the Japanese-style barbecue is its precision. There isn't a huge grate or any stacks of firewood or piles of charcoal here or there, there's no big ball filled with heat that escapes as soon as you open it. The skewers lie side by side, their ends resting on the sides of the grill box, and are turned one by one. You have everything within view and can take care of all the details.

By the way, you don't actually need to buy one. We built ours next to the fireplace using a few bricks. The only things that are really important is that it's long enough, that there's a correct distance between the charcoal and the food, and that the skewers rest on the edge.

This way you can do away with the typical grate, which is usually full of burnt fat and bits of meat from previous uses. The food is placed directly over the embers, which allows it to cook evenly.

The first time we sat in front of ours and grilled marinated mushrooms and spring onions, and tofu dengaku, there was something very satisfying and an almost meditation-like calm about it. We can only recommend you do the same.

Tip: Experiment with the skewers and the fat and juices that form on the vegetables. You can hold the skewers up at one end. You might even want to put the top of a pepper at the other end like a cup to collect the fat, leaving the vegetables light and airy. Or to collect the marinade, which caramelises and turns a beautiful dark colour, enhancing and refining its flavour.

GRILLED AUBERGINE

———◇◇◇———

As I was researching traditional Kaiseki cuisine, I came across a recipe in a cookbook on Zen temple cuisine that looked amazing. It was for an aubergine that was cut in half lengthways and then boiled or steamed. After lightly scoring the flesh, it was flavoured with a little soy sauce and ginger. There was nothing else to it. I could hardly imagine how it would taste prepared so simply. My previous experience with aubergines was of bitterly astringent objects with the consistency of polystyrene that are inedible raw and only made bearable with a lot of fat and strong-tasting ingredients like meat or tomatoes. You had to deep-fry or braise them, turning the insides to a mush, and the most recognisable flavour comes from the skin.

Until that time, steaming aubergines seemed an impossibility. In Japan, however, I quite often encountered them prepared this way. In one Kaiseki restaurant, the skin was even peeled off because the chefs were only interested in the consistency of the flesh. Pickled aubergine is eaten in Osaka, for which a certain type of aubergine is sliced raw and lightly brined.

What makes aubergine so different in Japan? First of all, it's very popular there and is one of the most important vegetables of the summer. There are said to be over sixty different varieties. In culinary terms, the Japanese aubergine is virtually diametrically opposed to our European aubergines. It holds its shape when cooked and become creamy at the same time. You can tell that it's actually a fruit whose pith tastes soft, juicy and sweetish, and that the individual chambers contain pith and seeds. This allows it to remain firm even after cooking, and it has a light consistency compared to European aubergines. When cooked, European aubergines turn into the opposite, becoming heavy and mushy, probably owing to their structural weakness. The taste of the Japanese aubergine is comparatively mild, sweet and rounded. And since it was actually grown in the neighbourhood where I stayed while conducting my 'field research' in Kyoto, it was – perhaps the most important thing of all – at its peak of ripeness.

GRILLED AUBERGINE

—◇◇◇—

However, we're not in Japan. What is one to do in this case? I'd avoid the polystyrene-like ones sold at supermarkets, whether organic or conventional, and look for aubergines in Asian or Oriental shops or at good greengrocers. The specimen we used for the recipe was purple and quite suitable.

The better – i.e. more defined, milder and more consistent – its taste, the easier it is to cook and it can be served more cleanly.

Aubergines are also very popular in Japan because they can be eaten cold and soaked in broth. They are quite fleshy and substantial, and they cool the mind and body in a delicious way.

In the traditional way, we serve the well-chilled aubergine with grated ginger in a little broth, and arranged quite simply in a glass bowl, which also conveys coolness.

Serves 2

1 medium (120–150-g), fruity-flavoured aubergine with little bitterness

Oil for brushing

150 ml kombu dashi

3 tbsp lemon juice

1 strip zest from an untreated lemon

1 tbsp light soy sauce

1 tbsp honey

2 pinches salt

1 tbsp lime juice (optional)

1 tsp freshly grated ginger

Brush the aubergine with oil and grill it whole over embers or bake in the oven at 180°C/350°F/gas 4 until soft and the skin wrinkles. Leave to cool down and then peel.

Mix all the remaining ingredients, except the ginger, and stir until smooth. Place the aubergine in a suitable container, pour over the broth and leave to stand for at least 1 hour, preferably overnight.

Cut the aubergine into pieces, season again with a little salt, if necessary, and garnish with the grated ginger. Serve well chilled.

CLEAR SUMMER VEGETABLE SOUP

—◇◇◇—

'What sort of soup do we want to make for summer?' Jule asked me. Then we thought: let's take things as they are. So Jule went through the garden and collected whatever was to be found there. These included yellow and red tomatoes, a moderately hot green chilli pepper, small green and purple peppers and a pumpkin flower.

The broth is made a little sweeter, which suits the soup quite well – surprisingly, because soups rarely have this nuance. The trick to all recipes, but especially the clear soups, is to experiment with the seasoning ingredients. The clear soup captures the taste of the treasures from the garden with its sweetness. And so a vivid impression of the summer is created through vegetables, just as it was that day.

This soup is meant to encourage you to take a walk through the garden or to the greengrocer's.

Serves 2

3–4 green beans
3–4 yellow beans
1 small pepper
50 g silken tofu
1 pumpkin or courgette
  flower
1 chilli pepper (we used a
  Peruvian lemon drop
  chilli pepper)
2–3 red and/or yellow
  cherry or baby plum
  tomatoes
500 ml kombu dashi
2 tsp sugar
2 tsp soy sauce
2–3 tsp mirin
2 tsp lemon juice
1 strip zest from an
  untreated lemon
1¾ tsp salt

Cut the beans into pieces and steam them for 2–3 minutes depending on their thickness (they should still be firm to the bite). Remove the stalk and seeds from the pepper, and cut it into thin rings. Halve or quarter the rings depending on size or preference. Cut the tofu into cubes. Cut off the bitter-tasting stem from the pumpkin or courgette flower. Cut two to three slices of the chilli pepper according to preference. Halve or quarter the tomatoes depending on their size.

Put the dashi into a pan and slowly bring to the boil. Add the sugar, soy sauce, mirin and lemon juice and zest. Taste the broth. Adjust the salt a little at a time, tasting again and again. It should have a balanced flavour tending towards sweet.

Add the pepper to the boiling broth. Then lower the heat, add the other ingredients and leave briefly so that they heat through. Taste the broth again. How is it for salt? Is it spicy enough and sweet enough? Remove the lemon zest and serve.

The flower and lemon drop chilli give our soup an aroma reminiscent of the Orient, with the light scent of jasmine and orchids, which is combined with the pungency of lemon and shrouded in sweetness.

AUBERGINES AND PEANUTS

———◇◇◇———

The summer settles in and temperatures rise. This is when we enjoy light and fresh things, although we're also happy to see hearty, creamy and strongly flavoured foods, especially when they're cool.

Aubergine goes well with fatty or oily accompaniments, in this case a thick coating of sauce made with dry-roasted and crushed peanuts.

Serves 2

2 small and narrow (about 150 g) aubergines

Oil for frying

50 g unsalted peanuts

3 tbsp kombu dashi

1 tsp light soy sauce

2–3 tsp lime juice

1 pinch salt

½ tsp sugar

A few thin strips of zest from an untreated lime

Cut the aubergines into thick slices. Heat about 2 cm of oil in a frying pan or small saucepan. Slowly fry the aubergine slices in the oil on both sides until soft and golden brown. Drain on kitchen paper.

Dry-roast the peanuts in a frying pan, then crush them to a coarse paste in a mortar (or use a blender, food processor or food chopper). Season with the dashi, soy sauce, lime juice, salt and sugar, and stir in the lime zest strips.

Mix the aubergines with the sauce and refrigerate. Serve well chilled on hot days.

SOYA BEANS, RED PEPPER AND LEMON

⸺◇◇◇⸺

Soya beans are often featured in the media and politics. They're considered a blessing and the answer to the world's problems by some, while others believe they're a thing of the past because of the environmental problems they cause.

In culinary terms, soya beans are somewhat overlooked. They're wonderfully smooth and therefore predestined to be turned into a cool summer dish. The same goes for peppers. These are pan-fried with the skin left so that its smoothness conveys a lovely sense of coolness. Very thin slices of lemon are added to give everything a kick of freshness. Is this the taste of summer?

Serves 2
50 g soya beans
½ (70-80 g) red pepper
1 untreated lemon
1 tbsp kombu dashi
1 tbsp mirin
1¼ tbsp sake
1 tbsp soy sauce
¾ tsp sugar

Soak the beans in water overnight to soften. On the day, cover with fresh water and cook according to the instructions on the packet until soft. They should always be covered with water. Then drain and leave to cool a little.

In the meantime, remove the stalk and seeds from the pepper and cut into quarters corresponding to its segments. Put the pepper quarters in a frying pan skin-side down, cover with a suitable lid and cook for 2–3 minutes. Allow to cool slightly and cut on a diagonal into strips.

Halve the lemon lengthways. Then cut 5 or 6 wafer-thin slices containing both skin and flesh.

Combine the dashi, mirin, sake, soy sauce and sugar and bring to the boil. Mix in the beans, pepper strips and lemon slices and marinate for at least 15 minutes.

This dish tastes good warm, but is at its best cold.

SESAME TOFU, NASTURTIUM AND PONZU

———— ◇◇ ————

Sesame tofu can be regarded as the 'signature dish' of Shojin Ryori, the cuisine of Zen Buddhist temples and monasteries. The general picture we have is that of novice monks sitting around what appeared to be a large mortar with many small grooves inside which they turned a wooden pestle in a circular motion to grind the sesame seeds to a paste, which was the basic component of sesame tofu. However, this preparation isn't tofu in the literal sense (because it isn't made from coagulated soya milk). The sesame paste is thickened with the starch made from the kuzu (or kudzu) root. You can also use potato starch if necessary, but the flavour won't be as good. Sesame tofu is considered something very precious and as such is served with the greatest simplicity, typically on its own and decorated only with a little grated wasabi.

Surprisingly, we found an echo of the flavour of wasabi when we sampled the nasturtiums in the garden. Of course, the flavours of wasabi and nasturtium are very different. However, the similarities lie in their complexity.

Both have a piquancy that is light and playful. Nasturtium is slightly sweetish and leaves room for other nuances of flavour.

This is how nasturtium found its way into this dish, and is it accompanied by an easy ponzu sauce, a dipping sauce made with citrus and soy sauce.

Serves 4
For the sesame tofu
200 ml water
25 g tahini (made from hulled white sesame seeds, e.g. from a whole food shop)
1 pinch salt
½–1 tsp sugar
20 g kuzu starch (potato starch if necessary, but it isn't a good substitute)

Mix the ingredients for the sesame tofu and bring to the boil over a medium heat, stirring constantly. Reduce the heat and cook, stirring constantly, until the mixture is shiny and the bottom of the pan can be seen for a few seconds while stirring. Rinse a small mould (e.g. a 250-g capacity tub) with water, pour in the mixture and leave to cool in a cold water bath until the tofu is firm. Cut into two to four portions. It's best to do this on a chopping board inside the water bath.

For the ponzu dipping sauce, mix the soy sauce with the lemon juice. Finely grind the lemon zest with the sugar in a mortar and add to the sauce.

Clean the nasturtium. Arrange the sesame tofu in a bowl, pour over the sauce and arrange the nasturtium around and on top of the tofu.

For the ponzu dipping sauce

4 tsp soy sauce

2 tsp lemon juice

2 fine and thin strips of zest from an untreated lemon

2 tsp sugar

Extras

1 handful of nasturtium leaves and, if possible, flowers

JAPANESE ANTIPASTI

———— ◇◇ ————

It was a balmy summer evening when we thought about preparing Japanese-style antipasti. What would that taste like? We imagined such a dish wouldn't be too far removed from the roasted and preserved pointed peppers that are so popular in the Balkans and wonderfully refreshing when well chilled.

So we grilled whole tomatoes and peppers from the garden. They can be prepared the day before or in the morning and then served cold in the sauce. Or they can be served directly. In this case, the dish works particularly well if you put some sauce and a piece of a vegetable on a spoon and put both in your mouth at the same time.

Serves 4

2 tomatoes (yellow, green, red, according to preference)
1 red pepper
1 yellow pepper
4 Padrón peppers (small green peppers)
Oil for rubbing

For the sauce

3 tbsp lemon juice
150 ml kombu dashi
1 tbsp light soy sauce
1 tbsp honey
Salt
1 strip zest from an untreated lemon
Sugar (according to taste, depending on the natural sweetness of the vegetables)

For the sauce, mix together lemon juice, dashi, soy sauce, honey and a few pinches of salt. Then add the lemon zest. Set aside in the refrigerator.

Rub the vegetables with oil and place them whole on the barbecue. Grill the tomatoes for 5-10 minutes, depending on their size; they will be well cooked by the time they burst. Char the peppers, except the Padrón peppers, on all sides until the skin turns black and loosens. Take them off the barbecue and leave to cool slightly. Then cut them open, remove the seeds and stalk and peel off the skin. Cut the flesh into thin wedges. Halve or quarter the tomatoes according to preference. Grill the Padrón peppers, turning regularly, until they are nicely coloured.

Depending on preference, put the cold vegetables into the sauce or arrange on a plate and pour over the sauce. If necessary, adjust the seasoning with a little salt or sugar. Then serve.

Tip: We also tried grilling a lemon and putting some of the fruit pulp in the sauce. However, lemon turns very bitter when it's grilled, so it's only worth the effort for the decorative effect.

COLD SOBA NOODLES WITH SPRING ONIONS AND TOMATO

Zaru soba, chilled soba noodles that you dip into an ice-cold, richly flavoured soup, is one of the most beautiful of Japanese dishes. Soba noodles are filling, delicious and easy to digest. They have a delicate flavour and lovely aroma. The soup, made with dashi, lots of mirin and soy sauce (the original is prepared with an extra measure of katsuobushi flakes) has a fascinating complexity. It is much too intense on its own, but when you dip the noodles in it and suck them both into your mouth at the same time, the resulting combination is exquisite.

The cold noodles and cold soup run down your throat and cool your body from the inside out, starting with the stomach, without being overly heavy.

That's what you want for summer: a richly flavoured, refreshing and yet light meal that is quick to prepare.

Serves 2

2–3 cherry or *baby plum tomatoes*

½ *spring onion*

240 g *dried soba noodles*

For the dipping soup

2 g *kombu kelp*

2 small (about 1-g) dried shiitake mushrooms

1 (4–5 g) dried tomato

40 ml soy sauce

40 ml mirin

2 tbsp sake

2 tsp sugar

For the soup, heat 160 ml water in a pan to about 60°C/140°F. Add the kombu, mushrooms and dried tomato and leave to steep at about the same temperature for at least 30 minutes. Then remove the mushrooms and kombu.

Add soy sauce, mirin, sake and sugar and bring to the boil. Leave to cool slightly. Take out the tomato, squeeze its juice into the soup and discard. Pour the soup into two wide cups that are as shallow as possible and refrigerate.

Halve the fresh tomatoes and cut into thin strips. Finely slice the spring onion.

Cook the soba noodles according to the instructions on the packet. NB: The higher the proportion of buckwheat flour, the better. The noodles are often a mixture of wheat and buckwheat. Drain the noodles in a sieve and – here's something we find quite unusual – wash them under running water to remove the sticky starch. This also cools the noodles down very quickly. Drain well, picking up and shaking the noodles by hand if need be. If the noodles are too wet, the soup will later become too watery and will not coat them properly.

Arrange the noodles in two bowls. Put some of the tomatoes and spring onions in each cup of dipping soup. Serve each bowl of noodles with a cup of the dipping soup. Pick up a portion of noodles with your chopsticks, dip them into the soup and slurp loudly.

APPLE AND CUCUMBER KIMCHI

—◇◇◇—

The idea for this recipe came from a recipe in my favourite cookbook for preparing tsukemono, fermented Japanese pickles. We tried it out, varied it, reduced it (the original also contains radishes) and were thrilled with the result because after just two or three hours in the refrigerator, there was a light, pleasant fermentation effect, which can't be guessed at just by looking at the ingredients. The vegetables are also eaten with their marinade. A quick and easy way to prepare an effective and refreshing dish to cool down on a balmy summer evening.

Serves 2

1 small (about 100-g) cucumber, as thin as possible

1 medium (about 120-g) apple

1 tbsp rice vinegar

1 tsp sugar

2 pinches salt

1 large piece of zest from an untreated lemon

1 piece fresh horseradish (to make 1 tsp chopped horseradish)

Slice the unpeeled cucumber. Halve and core the apple. Cut into wedges and then into slices of similar size to the cucumber slices. There should be equal amounts of cucumber and apple. Drizzle the apple pieces with a few dashes of vinegar.

Make the marinade by dissolving the sugar and salt in 100 ml of water. Cut the lemon zest into fine strips. Use a knife to finely chop about 1 teaspoon of horseradish. Combine the zest, horseradish and apple and cucumber pieces and mix with the marinade. Chill for 2–3 hours.

Serve in a chilled bowl with the marinade.

BROCCOLI WITH SESAME MUSTARD SAUCE

In Japan, the flower buds of the rape plant are typically eaten in spring. They are somewhat reminiscent of broccoli, whose many small buds seem to be on the verge of blooming. Rape buds and mustard are a popular combination in the Far East. We picked up on this and did the same with the broccoli. We serve the dish cold because it's summer. We give the dish a little kick with dark tahini made from roasted sesame seeds, which adds a creamy coating and emphasises its nuttiness.

Serves 2

120–130 g broccoli

For the sauce

2 tsp light soy sauce

2 tsp mustard (wholegrain, unsweetened)

1 tsp sugar

½ tsp dark tahini

2 tbsp water

Clean and cut the broccoli into florets, removing the hard parts from the stalks. Steam for 1½–2 minutes and refresh in plenty of cold water. Mix together the ingredients for the sauce. Add the broccoli, coat well and serve.

AUBERGINE AND COURGETTE DENGAKU

$\diamond\!\diamond\!\diamond$

Nasu dengaku is a classic dish that shouldn't be missing from any Japanese cookbook. Nasu is the Japanese word for aubergine. As previously described, it's one of the most popular summer vegetables in Japan, and it has also captivated us.

Nasu dengaku is aubergine glazed with a dengaku sauce made with sweetened miso paste. Before glazing, the aubergine can be cooked in different ways. We prefer to cook it on the barbecue because this allows it to develop delicate roasted aromas and flavour notes. The aubergine is glazed with a dark dengaku sauce. It's accompanied by a courgette glazed with a light dengaku sauce.

Serves 2

1 medium (180–200-g) aubergine
1 medium (150–200-g) courgette
Oil for brushing

For the light dengaku sauce

50 g white miso paste
1 tbsp sake
1 tbsp mirin
3 tbsp kombu dashi

For the dark dengaku sauce

50 g red miso paste
1 tbsp sake
1 tbsp mirin
1½ tbsp sugar
3 tbsp kombu dashi

For the light dengaku sauce, combine the ingredients, bring to the boil and allow to thicken to the original consistency of the miso paste. Stir constantly.

Repeat the process to make the dark glaze. The dark dengaku sauce needs a little sugar, while the light miso glaze is already sweet enough.

Remove the stalk and cut each of the vegetables in half lengthways. Score the flesh by making lots of diagonal incisions, resembling small diamonds. This keeps the vegetables juicy while they're being grilled.

We used our improvised Japanese barbecue and threaded two skewers each lengthwise into the aubergine and courgette. Grill the vegetables on both sides until cooked and the cut sides are golden brown. Make sure to skewer the vegetables as firmly to the skin as possible, as they become soft during grilling and could otherwise fall into the embers.

Then brush a thin coating of the light dengaku sauce over the cut surface of the courgette and a thin coating of the dark dengaku sauce over the cut surface of the aubergine. Grill on this side again until brown.

TWO-WAY PICKLED GHERKINS

———— ◇◇◇ ————

One of the features for which the Spree Forest, where this cookbook was conceived and born, is famous is a particular type of small gherkin, which is unfortunately only available outside the region for a short time each year, if at all. We were lucky to be able to source ours locally. They are a shiny dark green colour, turning a yellow-golden at the tip. Our actual idea was to subject them to a full preservation process, but part of the way in, after salting and sugaring, we discovered how good they taste fresh and raw.

We have chosen two ways of combining the pickled gherkins with the ginger: one that's fresh and tangy, and the other marinated for a deeper flavour. A well-made artisanal soy sauce is particularly worthwhile for this recipe. The higher their quality, the more delicate the flavour.

Serves 2

200 g gherkins

4 g salt (or 2 per cent of the weight of the cucumbers after cleaning)

2 tsp sugar

1 thumb-sized piece of ginger

1 tbsp soy sauce

1 tbsp sake

1 tbsp mirin

Rub the gherkins with the salt and 1 teaspoon of sugar and leave to stand for 30 minutes. Rinse quickly.

Cut the ginger into wafer-thin slices. Combine the soy sauce, sake and mirin, bring to the boil and remove from the heat. Add half the ginger slices. Cut half of the gherkins into about 2.5-cm-thick slices and add to the mixture. Transfer to a tall container or a resealable bag and marinate. The gherkin pieces must be completely covered with the marinade, otherwise turn them regularly. Refrigerate. They are ready to serve after 2 hours, otherwise marinate overnight.

For the fresh version, cut the other half of the ginger into fine strips, mix with 1 teaspoon of sugar and coarsely crush between your fingers. This will release the juice from the ginger. Roll the remaining whole gherkins in the crushed ginger. Leave to stand briefly and then cut into pieces. That's all there is to it.

Both versions are best served chilled.

MIRIN-PICKLED COURGETTES

——— ◇◇◇ ———

When we returned to the Spree Forest after a two-week break to cook up and photograph the summer dishes, we found the courgettes had run riot. Jule made her way through the wildly growing squash and courgette plants that had spread themselves around the garden like monsters, pulling thick green specimens out of a dense sea of leaves, calling out: 'Here's one... and here's another'. With our arms full, we returned to the kitchen. What could we do with so many of them? Most of them would be pickled using lacto-fermentation. However, we wanted to pickle a small number of them in a Japanese style.

To do this, we rubbed them with sugar and salt to remove a lot of their residual water, and then we marinated them in a special artisanal mirin. We also added a wholegrain mustard.

The courgettes began to glow as they pickled in the sweet wine, giving them an exquisite texture and complexity on the palate. A recipe for an evening where you might feel like having a special drop from the drinks cabinet.

Warning: this dish contains alcohol. To lessen the amount, bring the mirin marinade to the boil and remove from the heat.

If you like, you can add a few drops of a mild vinegar at the end, but literally only a few drops. Then the dish tastes like a delicate version of gherkins pickled with mustard seeds. However, we recommend not doing this. For this recipe you should use a very high-quality mirin.

Serves 5–6

250 g courgettes

2 tbsp salt

2½ tbsp sugar

3 tbsp mirin (highest quality)

2 tbsp wholegrain mustard

Halve the courgettes lengthways and scrape out the seeds. Although they can normally be marinated and eaten, we don't find them suitable for this recipe. Rub the courgettes with the salt and 1 teaspoon of sugar and stand upright in a bowl for 30 minutes so that the released liquid can drain off well.

Then cut into thick slices, mix with mirin, remaining sugar and mustard. Marinate for at least 1 hour, preferably overnight. Immediately before serving, season with a little salt.

TSUKEMONO

PICKLED SUMMER VEGETABLES
(TURNIPS AND RADISHES)

— ◇◇◇ —

In the section on spring we fermented kohlrabi and radishes – our aim in that case was to show that you can use the entire vegetable, including leaves and stems.

The first turnips also become available in the early summer. They still have a mild flavour and their tops are fresh-tasting. They are juicy and wonderfully refreshing, especially on hot summer days. Lightly fermented, they are full-bodied, tangy and fresh, minerally and a little sweet. What more could you want?

Serves 2

About 200 g small turnips and radishes

Salt (2 per cent of the weight of the vegetables after cleaning, about 4 g)

1 sheet (about 2 g) kombu kelp

2 tbsp rice vinegar

3 g demerara sugar

½ moderately hot chilli pepper

2 cherry leaves

Clean and weigh the turnips and radishes. Mix with 2 per cent of their weight in salt and the remaining ingredients. Seal tightly in a resealable bag or airtight container (see page 52). Put a weight on the bag or container and leave to ferment outdoors (this way is faster) or in the refrigerator (this takes longer). On warm and hot days, the first stage of the pickling process takes place after half a day to one full day, while this takes at least 24 hours or more in the refrigerator.

SHISO RICE

Shiso is very easy to grow, and the leaves we use are from our own crop. For some people, however, it quickly turns into a weed because it's so fast-growing and prolific. If it's too much of an effort to grow your own, shiso leaves are often found at Asian and Oriental shops.

Shiso here is also representative of a variety of things that can be mixed with the rice in this recipe, ranging from strips of nori seaweed and sesame seeds to chestnuts and grapes.

The unique aroma of the herb in this dish immediately takes me back me to Japan.

Serves 2

140 g round rice

3 green or red shiso leaves

Wash the rice thoroughly until the water runs clear (see page 56), drain and rest for 30 minutes. Then add 110 per cent of the weight of the rested rice in water.

Bring to the boil in a pan covered with a lid over a medium heat. Lower the heat as much as possible and continue cooking the rice until all the liquid has evaporated and it begins to crackle slightly in the pot.

Take off the lid, wipe the edges, cover the pan again and let the rice rest near the stove for at least 15 minutes. Cut the shiso leaves into thin strips and mix into the steamed rice.

BARLEY

The Japanese method of cooking rice isn't only suitable for buckwheat but also other cereals, such as barley or – in this recipe – naked barley, which is a variety with a loose and easily removed hull that doesn't require processing, allowing it to retain more nutrients.

We add a few more ingredients for flavour. They make the dish more substantial, and the smooth grains of barley take on a beautiful shine, giving extra pleasure to the mouth and the eye, especially when served chilled. Compared to white rice, barley is more original, although it isn't as adapted to our culinary preferences. It requires longer chewing, but has a lightness and airiness about it.

Serves 2

120 g naked barley

1 tsp soy sauce

1 tsp sake

1 pinch salt

Wash the naked barley until the water runs clear. Drain in a sieve and rest in the sieve or in a pan for 30 minutes.

Then weigh the barley and cover with 110 per cent of its weight in water. Add the soy sauce, sake and salt and cook the barley according to the instructions for white rice (see page 56). Bring to the boil over medium heat and cook for 10–12 minutes at low heat (or until you hear a light crackling sound and the water has evaporated). The lid can now be lifted and the edge of the pan wiped clean. Remove the pan from the heat, cover again with the lid and rest for 15–20 more minutes.

This barley can be enjoyed hot, at room temperature or cold.

RHUBARB TEMPURA WITH
LEMON AND ROSE SUGAR

Summer has begun and the rhubarb is still thriving in our garden. It's ready to be made into tempura. This time it will be a dessert, which is rather unusual, not only in Japan but also in our country.

But it's well worth it for the special feeling you get when the freshly fried rhubarb is dipped still hot into one of the flavoured sugars and then put into your mouth. The rhubarb is soft, aromatic, fragrant and sour, but the acidity is quickly countered by the sugar coating on the batter, and the flavour of lemon or rose hits the taste buds, making this small dish an intense summer pleasure.

Serves 2–3
2 medium rhubarb stalks
90 g plain flour
1 litre oil or *fat for deep-*
    frying

For the rose sugar
2–3 dried rose petals
2 tbsp demerara sugar
1 pinch salt

For the lemon sugar
1 strip zest from an
    untreated lemon
2 tbsp granulated sugar
1 pinch salt

Cut the rhubarb into finger-sized pieces, dust with the flour and set aside.

For the rose sugar, coarsely grind the dried rose petals in a mortar. Then add the demerara sugar and salt, grind again briefly and mix. Set aside.

For the lemon sugar, finely grind the lemon zest, granulated sugar and salt in a mortar – not for too long because the juice from the zest will cause the sugar to form clumps. Set aside.

Heat the oil to 180°C/356°F.

Line a bowl with ice packs and fill with water (or fill with ice water). Place a second bowl inside the first and add 140 ml of ice-cold water for the batter. When the oil has reached the desired temperature and everything else is ready, sieve the flour directly into the water. Use chopsticks to mix the batter coarsely and quickly; it should still have lumps.

Use chopsticks to dip the floured rhubarb pieces a little at a time, coating well in the batter, and put into the hot oil. Note: Every cooker, pot and pan, and every day is different. It is therefore best to control the temperature when deep-frying as it has a direct influence on the result. The temperature of the oil will remain steady if an appropriate size of pan and amount of oil are used, and if the right amount of rhubarb is put in to deep-fry.

When the bubbles in the oil become smaller and the bubbling dies down, the rhubarb is ready. Drain, serve with the two sugars and enjoy immediately.

ALMOND TOFU WITH BERRIES AND KUROMITSU

It's early summer, the first very small berries appear on the bushes, mainly raspberries, redcurrants and whitecurrants. We can't wait to make our way around the garden and pick them. Their supermarket counterparts, which we bought as a precaution for the photo shoot, look very old, even though they're twice as big and quite cute.

The first berries are given a place on an almond tofu made almost in the style of the famous sesame tofu of Zen monasteries. We say almost, because almond butter is used in order to make your work easier. The version made from fresh, blanched, peeled and finely ground almonds (gradually added to the water) is beautiful and aromatic, although it tends to be somewhat lumpier. When potato starch is used instead of the traditional kuzu starch, this type of tofu has a consistency similar to a custard pudding, although the outward resemblance is only slight.

East meets West somewhere in the middle of our creation. From Japan we have also borrowed kuromitsu, the dark sugar syrup. It coats the tofu and the fruit equally. The flavour of the berries alone shines through, finishing it off with a delicate hint of acidity.

Serves 2

40 g almond butter
5 tsp granulated sugar
2 pinches salt
20 g potato starch (from a wholefood shop)
20 g whole-cane sugar (e.g. muscovado sugar)
2 tablespoons berries, according to preference e.g. raspberries, redcurrants, whitecurrants, gooseberries

Mix the almond butter with 200 ml water, the granulated sugar, 1 pinch of salt and the starch until smooth and bring to the boil over a medium heat while stirring constantly. Lower the heat and continue stirring until the mixture is shiny and the bottom of the pan can be seen for a second or two when a spatula is run through it.

Rinse a small mould (e.g. a 250-g capacity tub) with water, pour in the mixture and leave to cool in a cold water bath until the tofu is firm.

Combine the whole-cane sugar, 1 pinch of salt and 10 ml water and bring to the boil, stirring until the sugar has dissolved. The resulting sugar syrup is known as kuromitsu (literally the Japanese for 'black honey').

Cut into two to four portions. It's best to do this on a chopping board inside a water bath. Arrange the almond tofu in a bowl, garnish with the berries and pour over the kuromitsu. Ideal for the first hot summer days.

REICHA SENCHA

—◇◇◇—

Reicha is the Japanese word for iced tea. Many varieties of tea can be used, such as genmaicha (also known as popcorn tea), mugicha (barley tea) – which we later present in the chapter on autumn as a hot beverage – and sencha (green tea) which we present here. These teas are enjoyed both hot and cold in Japan. There are countless vending machines to be found all over the country. A blue lamp on one of these machines indicates cold tea, while a red lamp signals that hot tea is available.

Green tea is said to have a cooling effect on the body. This effect can be further enhanced by serving the tea cold. Cold tea is very simple to make: pour tea leaves into a bottle, add water and refrigerate overnight. It's ready to enjoy the next day. If you don't want to wait that long, you will already have a good result after two hours.

We recommend the use of organic tea because it's grown with less fertiliser, resulting in a more delicate and balanced flavour. Tea prepared the conventional way can develop a somewhat intrusive umami richness. Since cold extraction is used here, simple teas that become bitter more quickly with high water temperatures or whose flavour is in the stems are very suitable for reicha.

Serves 2

*1 tbsp organic sencha
   (green tea)*
500 ml filtered water

Put the tea leaves in a bottle, fill it up with the filtered water, cover with a lid and refrigerate for at least 2 hours. Stir or gently shake the bottle once before serving. Strain directly into the glass.

UJIKINTOKI KAKIGORI

MATCHA-FLAVOURED SHAVED ICE WITH RED BEANS AND RICE CAKES

This dessert is a special treat on hot days, which is why it's so popular with the Japanese. Even if the composition may seem a little strange to the Western palate, the ingredients are exactly the same as those featured in the tea ceremony, only prepared and combined differently. Here, the matcha is poured over the shaved ice in the form of a syrup. It is served with anko and rice cakes, known as mochi – although the red bean paste is typically used as a filling for these cakes – and served as wagashi, the traditional sweets of the tea ceremony.

The effect is impressive. When eating a small bowl of this dessert, you can feel the coolness moving down your gullet and deep into your stomach. It cools from the inside out in a way that ice cream simply can't.

In the original version, large, old-fashioned, hand-operated machines are used to shave whole blocks of ice into a fine snow-like texture. It is said that snow in Japan was once stored in caves until the summer, when it was flavoured and served to the nobility as a dessert.

Serves 2

4 tsp anko (see page 65)

For the matcha syrup

15 g sugar
3 g matcha
1 pinch salt

For the rice cakes

30 g glutinous (sticky) rice flour

Freeze 200 ml of water in a plastic container, preferably overnight in the freezer, or use the same amount of crushed ice or ice cubes.

Chill two bowls. Cook the anko according to the recipe on page 65. For the matcha syrup, bring water to the boil and pour 15 ml of boiling water over the sugar. Stir to dissolve. Leave to cool slightly, then sift 3 g of matcha through a fine sieve into the syrup and stir in. Season with the salt.

For the rice cakes, very slowly stir very small amounts of water into the rice flour and then knead to a smooth and sticky dough. Roll the dough into a sausage, divide into six lengths with small incisions and with moistened hands twist off small dumpling-shape cakes.

Heat about 500 ml water in a small pan and keep just below boiling point. Put the dumplings into the boiling water and wait until they float to the surface.

Put the block of ice or ice cubes into a bag and smash into small pieces with a hammer. Then put it into a blender and finely grind. Divide the ice between the two chilled bowls and pour over the matcha syrup. Add three rice cakes and 2 teaspoons of anko to each bowl and serve immediately.

AUTUMN

WHAT IS AUTUMN?

There is a different sound to this season. You notice the change as autumn approaches. While in summer there's a great deal of humming and buzzing and the singing of birds, the sounds of autumn are more indirect. The leaves rustle. They're soft in summer and the wind blows through them. But as they wither, they harden and suddenly resonate more.

'Plop' and 'thud' go the chestnuts when they fall on the roof, on the stones in front of the house and on the dry grass. And in between you hear silence and the feeling grows that something is over; it has come to an end.

This is the gentle melancholy that autumn brings, despite being a time of joy and fruit. The days shorten, and morning brings the first hoarfrost to the meadows. Energy changes its direction. It has been flowing outwards so far. Now it retreats and heads inwards.

The main activity is gathering. The fruits of the year often ripen at the same time. Things come to fruition and are found in abundance. In our culture we've always had a special way of thinking about tomorrow – about the long winter and even longer spring, until the first vegetables emerge from the ground in May or June.

Autumn is the gold of the leaves and the low-lying sun. But it's also rainy November, when each recollection of warm and sunny days makes us glad. Autumn is both a time for feasting and for thinking about transience and tomorrow.

FIG, WHITE MISO AND MINT

———◇◇◇———

Back when I was in Kyoto, I once ate a dish of fig in miso at the Kikunoi Kaiseki restaurant, which came with katsuobushi and a little mustard. I was very impressed by the dish at the time, and I had been looking forward all summer to finding my own way to make fig in miso. My version does away with the katsuobushi and the mustard, and it has been greatly simplified.

The dish now has a light hint of lemon and the subtle freshness of mint. For me it's like late summer or early autumn: sweetness, creaminess and ripeness. The added freshness and acidity both hint at the change of seasons and satisfy the need for refreshment on the warm and golden days at this time of the year.

Serves 2
3 ripe red or green figs
½ tsp sugar
3 tbsp kombu dashi
1 tbsp white miso paste
3 tsp sake
½ tsp lemon juice
1 strip zest from an
   untreated lemon
2 -3 small mint leaves

Cut the figs in half. In a small pan, cook the sugar to a light caramel and lay the figs cut-side down in the pan. Leave to stand for 20 seconds and then take them out. Add the other ingredients except the mint, to the pan and stir until smooth. Bring to the boil and then reduce slowly until the sauce is creamy. Remove the pan from the heat and leave to cool.

Put the figs and the mint in a tall container (I like to use a resealable bag) and pour the sauce over the top (if the miso still has chunks, strain through a sieve first). Marinate for at least 1 hour in the refrigerator.

SWEETCORN SOUP
WITH SILKEN TOFU

———— ◇◇◇ ————

A sweetcorn soup? Jule and I were discussing the dishes we would be making over the next few days. She had picked two ears of sweetcorn and had been badgering me about a sweetcorn soup for days.

I wondered what could be so Japanese about that. I had neither seen nor eaten anything like it during my time there.

When the soup was finally in front of us and the photos taken, we calmly tried it. I was blown away. It tasted very Japanese in a certain sense, namely in that it tasted of the sweetcorn itself. And it's also quickly and easily prepared using five basic ingredients.

The silken tofu accentuates the silkiness of the soup. At the same time, the sweetcorn cakes bring back to the soup the smoothness and sweetness of the kernels that are lost during the puréeing process.

Serves 2

1 ear sweetcorn
500 ml kombu dashi
1 tsp light soy sauce
Salt
60 g silken tofu
½ tsp flour
Oil for frying

Remove the husk from the sweetcorn and steam the cob for 1–2 minutes. Use a knife to cut the kernels from the cob (this is best done by holding the cob upright on a dish). Set aside 2 tablespoons of corn kernels.

Bring the dashi to the boil, add the corn kernels and cook for 1–2 minutes. Purée the soup and strain through a sieve. Return to the pan and keep warm over a low heat. Season with the soy sauce and about half a teaspoon of salt. Our soup is naturally sweet.

Cut the tofu into about 2.5-cm cubes and heat through in the soup.

Mix the flour with half a teaspoon of water. Add the previously set aside sweetcorn kernels. Heat about 2 cm of oil in a frying pan. Use two tablespoons to shape the kernels into two small cakes and fry in the oil. This should take 1–2 minutes, turning over halfway through. Season lightly with salt.

Put the soup into a bowl, arrange the tofu and sweetcorn cakes in the soup and serve.

TOMATOES AND YUBA

—◇◇◇—

Yuba is one of the most beautiful products found in Japanese cuisine. It is the skin that forms on the surface of soya milk when heated. There are yuba-makers in Kyoto who have been making this product by hand every day for many generations and delivering it to good restaurants.

Yuba is best fresh. Its consistency is a little reminiscent of that of mozzarella. In order to acquaint you with it, we have designed this dish in a similar way with ripe tomatoes straight from the garden and with a tangy dressing.

Now comes the 'but': it's the only recipe where you'll have difficulty finding the basic ingredients. I brought back dried yuba with me from my last trip to Kyoto. While it's good, it doesn't compare to the fresh product. You can get a little taste of yuba by buying the Chinese version, known as dried bean curd skin or tofu sheets. Although it's also a very interesting and beautiful-looking product, it's unfortunately only a substitute.

The next step would be to give tofu makers a push or convince a flight attendant to bring some back for you. You can even make it yourself on the stove: just find a tutorial on YouTube or wait for our next book to come out. Or you can just go to Kyoto.

Serves 2

1 large tomato

1 small tomato

10 yuba rolls (imported from Kyoto; alternatively Chinese dried bean curd skin from an Asian or Oriental shop)

4 tsp lime juice

2 tsp light soy sauce

2 tsp sugar

Cut the tomatoes into slices. Bring 200 ml water to the boil. Remove from the heat, add the yuba and soak for 15 minutes, or until soft. Then take the yuba out and carefully squeeze to drain.

Mix the lime juice with the soy sauce and sugar to make a dressing. Arrange the tomato slices, yuba rolls and the dressing on a plate, either separately or like a classic Caprese salad.

This dish is also ideal served cold on warm autumn days.

Tip: The dried yuba becomes soft faster if a pinch of baking soda is added to the water. This reduces the soaking time to about 5 minutes. Then carefully squeeze out the water as described in the recipe and continue to use.

GRAPES AND WALNUTS

———◇◇◇———

Is this dish a snack for between meals? That's right; it's like a prelude to autumn. And at the same time, its colours, aesthetics and flavour essentially reflect what is so special about this season.

In the forest, the walnuts lie so thickly scattered in the grass under the trees next to the house that it's difficult not to hear them crunching under our feet. The wild boar would love to get at them. They have already churned up the paths all around here in search of this delicate nut.

This time of year brings to mind a dish from the Kikunoi Kaiseki restaurant that I was unfortunately never able to try: Muscat grapes marinated in koji. We found our own way of capturing the essence of autumn with wine and nuts.

Serves 2

For the grapes

1 tsp sake

1 tsp mirin

1 tsp shio koji (koji marinade)

½ tsp light soy sauce

50 g red and white grapes

For the walnuts

40 g shelled walnuts

1 tsp sugar

2 tbsp sake

½ tsp regular soy sauce

1 pinch salt

Mix the sake, mirin, shio koji and light soy sauce and marinate the grapes in the mixture for at least 1 hour, preferably overnight.

Dry-roast the walnuts in a frying pan over a medium heat, turning from time to time. Peel off as much skin as possible. You can also put the walnuts in a cloth and carefully rub them against each other. Be Zen about it: it doesn't have to be perfect.

Cook the sugar to a light caramel in a small saucepan. Then lower the heat, add the nuts and deglaze with the sake. Reduce a little, then add the soy sauce, toss and season with a little salt.

Remove the grapes from their marinade and serve with the walnuts. A small snack it may be, but it's the essence of autumn.

BRUSSELS SPROUTS
WITH CHILLI

——◇◇◇——

The nicest thing you can do with Brussels sprouts is to bake or fry them so that they lose a little water, become more intense and sweet and acquire roasted notes. It all goes hand in hand, and it's all very simple. We decided to fry them because it saves energy and you can see what you're doing. When frying, you have to be careful to colour the Brussels sprouts slowly and evenly.

Serves 2

10 (about 200 g) Brussels
*   sprouts*
1–2 tbsp sesame oil
2–3 mild to medium
*   hot chilli peppers,*
*   depending on preference*
Salt

Halve the Brussels sprouts. Steam for 1½–2 minutes. The cooking time will also depend on the size of the individual sprouts.

Heat the sesame oil in a frying pan and add the Brussels sprouts cut-side down. Fry for 2–3 minutes over a medium heat, and then turn over and continue to fry until golden brown. Add the chillies (we used a very small, mild variety grown in the garden) and toss.

Season with salt and serve immediately.

Tip: The dish can be given a finishing touch with 1–2 teaspoons of toasted sesame seeds.

It also goes well with lightly cooked quince. To do this, remove the core from 1 small (120–130 g) quince and cut into wedges. Cook sugar to a caramel and deglaze with sake, soy sauce and a little water. Add the quince wedges to the mix and cook over a moderate heat until soft. Season with salt and sugar and serve with the Brussels sprouts.

JERUSALEM ARTICHOKES
WITH MISONNAISE

———◇◇◇———

All summer long, whenever we passed the bright yellow Jerusalem artichoke flowers, we'd be looking forward to the time the first tubers would be ready. Once we even tried the tubers in August, but they were inedible; their skin was still quite bitter, probably to keep predators away.

But now was the right time. Jule started digging and pulled out several delicate objects from the loosened soil. After a short taste test, we decided to do as little as possible with them. The skin would be lightly enhanced with the simple and wonderful combination of sugar and soy sauce; when grilled over the embers, it gives off an appealing aroma reminiscent of the smell of freshly baked bread. This smell reminds me of Kyoto and the narrow streets of Gion, the old entertainment district, where all kinds of things are left to sizzle on the grill in the evening.

The tubers are accompanied by a mayonnaise that is mixed in the traditional way. We use the soya lecithin in place of egg.

For anybody who hasn't made mayonnaise before, you'll need a strong arm and a lot of patience. For us, however, this fits in well with the Zen way. Mayonnaise involves joining two things that won't come together by themselves: oil and water. However, if you build them a bridge, they enter into a wonderful, creamy and harmonious union.

Should the sauce split or curdle as you make it, don't despair. Start the process again with some mustard and miso paste, and then add the curdled sauce again a spoonful at a time, stirring constantly, with an empty mind and a loose hand.

JERUSALEM ARTICHOKES WITH MISONNAISE

————◇◇◇————

Serves 2

1 tbsp demerara sugar

1 tbsp soy sauce

*130–150 g Jerusalem
    artichokes*

For the misonnaise

*Zest from ½ an untreated
    lemon*

½ tsp mustard

2–3 dashes lemon juice

1 tsp white miso paste

6 tbsp neutral oil

Finely crush the sugar in a mortar. Mix with the soy sauce.

Build a Japanese-style barbecue (or use a normal barbecue instead) and light it (see Method for grilling, page 72).

For the misonnaise, cut the lemon zest into very thin julienne strips and grind into a paste in a mortar. Combine the mustard, lemon juice and miso paste in a large bowl and mix in a circular motion using a whisk or electric hand mixer. Add the oil, first incorporating one drop at a time, then one teaspoon at a time and finally one tablespoon at a time. This can be time-consuming – sometimes taking up to 15 minutes – but it's well worth the effort. And you can focus your concentration on the essential action of mixing.

Brush the Jerusalem artichokes with the sugar and soy sauce mixture. Thread them onto metal skewers and grill over the embers until crispy on all sides. Brush again with the mixture if you like. This will make the flavour of the skin more intense. Don't let the tips of the tubers turn too dark.

Dip the still hot Jerusalem artichokes in the misonnaise and enjoy.

THE PEAR AS A PEAR

———◇◇◇———

'Have you actually been influenced by Japan?' was a question I was asked time and time again. 'Yes,' I would answer, 'It pretty much left me with my hands tied at first.' How could I – after having trained in fine-dining cuisine and could make parfaits, forcemeat, jus and other things – continue to cook when these things no longer seemed appropriate to me? One of the loveliest things that guided me on the path to finding a different way of cooking was a pear.

At the time I asked myself the question: what is the essence of a pear? That's when I realised that a pear is a diva, because it only reveals its full splendour when ripe, before it quickly gets bruised, turns mushy, oxidises and goes brown. If it's to be served in all its beauty, it has to be handled delicately and treated very well. Then it rewards the cook and displays the depth of its quality.

This is the way I found to serve the pear as a pear. Peel the pear and make a poaching liquid with the skin. Let the naked pear steep and marinate in the liquid and then serve. It needs nothing but itself. A diva.

THE PEAR AS A PEAR

———◇◇◇———

Serves 2

1 untreated lemon

2 (about 100-g) pears or
    4 small (about 50-g)
    pears

2–3 tbsp sugar, depending
    on the ripeness of the
    pears

1–2 pinches salt

Demerara sugar

5 g kuzu starch
    (alternatively, potato
    starch or cornflour)

Peel and halve the lemon. Set aside the rind. Squeeze the juice and put into a large bowl.

Peel the pears. Use a melon baller to scoop out their cores through the bottom. Set aside both the peels and cores. If using small pears, keep whole. If using large pears, halve them. Dip the peeled pears in the lemon juice to keep from turning brown.

Cook the sugar to a dark caramel in a saucepan. Add the pear peels and cores of the pears, and then add water. Now comes the difficult part: there should be enough liquid left after cooking to cover the pears later. I find that 200 ml does the trick. Heat everything to just below boiling.

Add the pears, reduce the heat and poach until just tender, like asparagus. Depending on ripeness and size, this will take between 8 and 20 minutes. Like I said: diva. Turn the pears once in this time. Use a knife to check if they're done by inserting the tip into a pear. If it slides in and out easily, it's cooked.

Transfer the pears to a tall container. Reduce the liquid to 200 ml. Add the lemon rind to the cooking liquid. Season with the salt and demerara sugar. The liquid can be a little too sweet but the pears will make up for this.

Bring the liquid to the boil. Dissolve the starch in 1–2 tablespoons of water and stir into the liquid. Bring the liquid back to the boil, remove from the heat and leave to cool down a little. Pour it over the pears.

The pears should be left in the liquid for a whole day.

Tip: The preserved pears go well with the chestnut sweets on page 156.

YELLOW BEETROOT, HIJIKI AND TOFU

———◇◇◇———

Hijiki seaweed combines well with sweet flavours. It's prepared in this way in Japan, often accompanied with soya beans and carrots, giving it a somewhat shiny, rich, almost liquorice-like quality. And a very satisfying flavour.

The yellow beetroot have a similar quality. They are also rich and shiny, and their earthy sweetness produces a lovely feeling in mouth and stomach.

Serves 2

5 g dried hijiki seaweed

30 g deep-fried tofu (available at Asian or Oriental shops)

8 tbsp kombu dashi

3 tbsp sake

1 ½ tsp sugar

2 tbsp mirin

2 ½ tbsp soy sauce

Soak the seaweed in water for 20 minutes. Cut the tofu into thin strips. Soak in hot water for a short time and drain. Peel and slice the beetroot and steam for about 20 minutes.

Drain the seaweed and discard the soaking water. Combine the seaweed with the dashi and bring to the boil. Add the tofu, sake, sugar, mirin and soy sauce and simmer for 7–10 minutes, covered. Remove the lid and reduce the sauce. Stir in the beetroot and serve.

POTATOES WITH POPPY SEEDS

———◇◇◇———

'Mmmh, yummy!' During our time in the Spree Forest, there were always children running around us and getting in the way while we were cooking and taking pictures.

There was one particular day, however, when the children watched us work for a while, waiting anxiously for the results. We had asked a boy the day before to go into town to get us some potatoes. So, naturally, he now wanted to know what happened to them.

The potatoes, neat and simple, covered in black and white poppy seeds and seasoned with just a few salt flakes, were finally set before the children. And no sooner were they inside their mouths than there came a chorus of voices exclaiming 'yummy!'

Those who haven't given up hope that there's more to delight children's hearts than pasta with tomato sauce can prepare this dish together with them. It's sure to be a success.

Serves 2

5–6 baby potatoes
200 ml kombu dashi
1 tsp light soy sauce
1 tsp mirin
Salt
2 tbsp flour
1 pinch sugar
3 tbsp black poppy seeds
3 tbsp white poppy seeds
Oil for frying
Salt flakes for serving

Peel and halve the potatoes. Cook them in the dashi (if they aren't covered by the liquid, cover the pan with a lid and turn the potatoes from time to time) together with the light soy sauce, mirin and 1–2 pinches of salt until tender. Leave to cool down a little.

Mix the flour with 2 tablespoons of water to a thick batter (similar to pancake batter) and season lightly with 1 pinch each of salt and sugar. Put the black and white poppy seeds into separate bowls.

Dip the potatoes in the batter. Coat half in the black poppy seeds and the other half in the white poppy seeds.

Heat about 2 cm of oil in a small frying pan. Fry potatoes on all sides. Drain briefly on kitchen paper or in a sieve. Sprinkle with salt flakes and serve.

WALNUT TOFU WITH PLUMS

AND MUSTARD/WALNUT TOFU WITH SOY SAUCE

This dish looks a bit like a Western dessert – something creamy served with fruit – except for the mustard and walnut tofu made without dairy products, which we would typically expect a dessert like this to contain.

Plums and walnuts are plentiful in the early autumn, so it's only natural to combine them. And the mustard should be hot and pungent because it gives body to the dish. The heat rises through the creaminess of the walnut and the thick skin of the plum mantle, bringing together and lifting the flavour, and then lingers. This creates a trio of flavours somewhere between sweet and savoury in a very small space.

What would a Japanese Kaiseki chef say to that? Would there already be too much complexity in the dish? And where's the walnut? Can it still be tasted? To experience this by itself, the walnut tofu should be served only with soy sauce. This coats the tofu not only visually, but also in terms of taste. As if by a miracle (in fact, it is probably the flavour-enhancing properties of the soy sauce), the flavour of walnut clearly comes through. Then the idea behind these tofu-like preparations – whether made from sesame, almonds or walnuts – can be understood, as well as that of the soy sauce, because both serve to bring out the best in their own flavour.

The question of which dish is better is left to you and your taste. Both are coherent in themselves and are very close to each other. 'Not only but also, and all things are incomparable.'

WALNUT TOFU WITH PLUMS
AND MUSTARD/WALNUT TOFU WITH SOY SAUCE

———◇◇◇———

Serves 2

25 g shelled walnuts
20 g kuzu starch
1 pinch salt
1 pinch sugar

Either:

100 g plums
2 tsp sugar
1 pinch salt
About 6 tbsp sake
1 g kuzu starch
½ tsp hot mustard
 (e.g. Dijon mustard)
1 dash mirin

Or:

2–3 tsp light soy sauce

Dry-roast the walnuts, put them in a cloth and rub them against each other. This loosens a large part of the bitter skin in the process. You don't need to be too fussy; eighty per cent is enough, as they say in Zen Buddhism. A slightly bitter note isn't such a bad thing after all.

Finely crush the kernels in a mortar. Mix with the kuzu starch and 200 ml of water. Press through a sieve according to preference. Put the mixture into a pan and bring to the boil while stirring constantly. Continue to cook over a moderate heat, stirring constantly, until the mixture is thick and shiny and the bottom of the pan can be seen for a few seconds while stirring. Season carefully with 1 pinch of salt and 1 pinch of sugar. Pour into moulds (e.g. empty 250-g capacity tubs). Put the moulds into a cold water bath and leave to cool.

In the meantime, pit and quarter the plums. Cook the sugar to a caramel. Add the plums, salt and 4 tablespoons of sake. Cook over a low heat for 1 minute. Mix the kudzu starch with 2 tablespoons of sake and stir into the plums. Cook briefly until the mixture thickens and then remove from the heat.

For the mustard sauce dots, mix half a teaspoon of hot mustard with 1 dash of sake and 1 dash of mirin.

Turn out the walnut tofu onto a chopping board and cut it into two or four portions, depending on your appetite. Garnish with a dot of mustard sauce and serve with the plums.

For the simpler version, prepare the walnut tofu as described, pour over with the soy sauce and serve.

LACTIC ACID-FERMENTED CARROTS AND BEETROOT

A large number of different fermentation methods are used to pickle vegetables in Japan. However, I never encountered lactic acid fermentation in my time there. It's a very simple process and actually only needs time and a little care.

It's good to touch the vegetables when we are preparing them because the bacteria that lives on our skin will be transferred to them and give the vegetables our unmistakable taste.

Oak leaves contain tannins that keep the vegetables firm and crispy. You can also use cherry leaves (see pages 52 and 100), redcurrant leaves or classic vine leaves.

Feel free to add spices (juniper, pepper, cinnamon, even rose petals) or onions.

This basic approach allows many different vegetables to be pickled using lactic acid fermentation.

Serves 2

2 (200–250 g) carrots
3 small (250 g) beetroot
6 slices ginger
4 oak leaves
Salt

Carefully wash the unpeeled carrots and peel the beetroot. Cut the vegetables according to preference. I prefer to cut the carrots into batons and the beetroot into wedges.

Put the vegetables separately into resealable bags, each with 3 slices of ginger and 2 oak leaves. Place a bowl on kitchen scales and set to zero using the tare function. One at a time, put an open bag on the scales and add enough water to cover the vegetables. Calculate two per cent of the total weight in salt and add it to the bag.

Seal the bags, leaving a small gap. Then press out the air and seal fully. Keep the bags in a cool, dark place, preferably in a small container because they can sometimes overflow.

At the beginning, check progress at least once a day and squeeze out any air. This 'care' routine allows you to observe and helps you to control the natural fermentation process.

Things come to life after 2–3 days. Now you can release the gas produced by the fermentation process several times a day. After 14 days (at typical autumn temperatures) the vegetables will have reached the stage where they develop their peak flavour. The fermentation process slows down. In order to slow it down completely and to store the pickled vegetables, simply keep them in the refrigerator, either in their bag or transferred to a clean jar. The only really essential thing is to always keep the vegetables covered in the brine, otherwise they will spoil.

The vegetables will keep for up to a year and develop a deep and rich flavour.

MISO SOUP
WITH WHITE ONION

———◇◇◇———

This soup is delicate and restrained, and easy to make. What is so special about it is that the onion is lightly seasoned with salt and sugar and cooked slowly. During the process, its juice is released, evaporates, and caramelises, and its flavour intensifies from within. The onion as an onion. So, if you dedicate time to its preparation, it will practically cook itself and you will be richly rewarded. You discover one side of a vegetable that develops with patience and mindfulness, like a good bread made from dough that has been allowed to rise slowly. This is just an example. More vegetables are waiting to be discovered in this way.

Serves 2

1 (140–160-g) mild-
   flavoured white onion
½ tsp sugar
Oil for frying
1 pinch salt
500 ml kombu dashi
2 tbsp sake
2 tsp mirin
40 g white miso paste

Slice the onion into thin rings. Cut the larger rings in half and leave the smaller ones whole. Cook the sugar to a light caramel in a pan and add the onion, salt and oil. Cook the onion over a medium heat, half-steaming and half-frying, until translucent and soft. This should take 10–12 minutes. Stir occasionally.

Pour off the oil, add the dashi, sake and mirin, and slowly bring the soup to the boil. Finally, put the miso paste into a sieve, hold the sieve inside the soup and press through with a spoon. The soup should not be boiling.

Best served in a lacquer or wooden bowl to keep the soup hot.

WINTER SQUASH AND MISO SOUP WITH RICE CAKES

———◇◇◇———

Attentive readers will have noticed that miso soup is featured twice. The first is with white onion, while this version is to celebrate winter squash because it's getting noticeably cooler, and because winter squashes and pumpkins illuminate everything so beautifully and bring joy. It comes as no surprise to us that orange is considered a cosmic and spiritual colour in Buddhism. We put three little moons – rice cakes, known as mochi – in each bowl of soup to remind us of the three beautiful full moons of autumn.

Serves 2

160–200 g winter squash (e.g. red kuri squash)
500 ml kombu dashi
30 g glutinous (sticky) rice flour
2 tsp sake
25–30 g white miso paste
Salt

Cut the squash into pieces. Combine with the dashi in a pan. You can also add the seeds and fibres. Bring to the boil and cook, covered, over a medium heat until soft.

In the meantime, add water a teaspoon at a time to the rice flour until it forms a dough and shape into six dumpling-like cakes. As you will see, sticky rice lives up to its name. It helps to wet your fingers.

Bring water to the boil and cook the rice cakes until they float to the surface, by which time they're cooked. NB: Rice cakes tend to stick to the bottom of the pan. You should swirl the water when adding.

Take the rice cakes out of the pan. Heat a small frying pan without adding oil and toast the rice cakes on both sides until brown.

Strain the soup through a fine sieve, pressing the squash through with a ladle or spoon. The soup thickens by itself and should be nice and creamy. If it's too thick, add dashi or water.

Put the soup back into the pan and slowly warm it up again. Add the sake. Put the miso paste into a sieve, hold the sieve inside the soup and press through with a spoon. Taste the soup and adjust the seasoning with salt if necessary.

Pour the soup into two bowls and serve with three toasted rice cakes in each.

RICE WITH CHANTERELLES

———◇◇◇———

Sometimes more is better. A generous portion of chanterelle mushrooms is good for this dish. But this dish will work even if only a small amount is available and you practise the Japanese way of paring everything down to the essentials.

The rice makes all the difference. It's so clean and neutral that it brings out the flavour of the mushrooms particularly well. And by steaming and allowing the rice to swell with the lid on, none of their flavour is lost. This combination is refined by the sweetness of mirin and the complexity of sake and soy sauce.

This is for me one of the simplest and most beautiful dishes in our book. It can be made using almost any sort of mushroom and many other vegetables.

Serves 2

50–70 g chanterelle
    mushrooms

140 g rice

2 tbsp sake

1 tsp light soy sauce

1 tsp salt

2 tbsp mirin

Wipe the mushrooms clean with a cloth or brush.

Wash the rice according to the basic recipe on page 56, leave to rest and add 110 per cent of the weight of the rested rice in water. Mix in the mushrooms, sake, soy sauce, salt and mirin. Bring to the boil over a medium heat. Then reduce the heat to the lowest setting. Continue to cook the rice until all the water has been absorbed and evaporated (you can tell by the crackling sound coming from the pan).

Turn off the heat and rest the rice for 15 more minutes. Lift the lid and enjoy the smell and sight of the mushrooms and rice. Serve.

RICE WITH PORCINI MUSHROOMS, NORI AND CELERY

Nowhere is paring things down to the essentials more beautiful than with rice. I experienced this time and again in Japan, where a meal isn't considered to be complete until the rice is served.

Even today when the side dishes accompanying rice almost almost seem to have become more important, rice can still be a complete meal in itself and only needs to be supplemented with a few ingredients.

Among the most beautiful things used to adorn it are mushrooms, such as matsutake ('pine mushroom') in Japan and as porcini mushroom for us.

What more could you want than a bowl of rice garnished with mushrooms and two or three other things? A fine pleasure in all its simplicity.

Serves 2

140 g rice

1 sheet nori

2–3 sticks celery

1 (30–40-g) porcini mushroom

Oil for frying

1 dash lemon juice

Salt

1 tsp sake

Prepare and cook the rice according to the basic recipe on page 56.

Use scissors to cut the nori sheet horizontally into very thin strips. Cut the celery sticks into 4–5-cm lengths.

Clean the mushroom, preferably without water, wiping only with a cloth or brushing, and cut into about 1½–cm–thick slices. Heat a little oil in a frying pan and fry over a high heat until golden brown on both sides. Drizzle with the lemon juice. Stir the mushrooms briefly to coat with the juice and remove from the pan. Season with a few grains of salt.

Lower the heat, add the sake and celery to the pan and cover with a lid. Sweat for 1–2 minutes.

Put the rice in two bowls, arrange the mushroom slices and celery pieces on top and garnish with the nori strips before serving. Optionally, stir once with chopsticks before eating.

TOFU, HAZELNUT AND CAPE GOOSEBERRIES

Under a covering of cape gooseberries and hazelnuts, the tofu is almost turned into a cream of the sort we appreciate so much in Europe. This is therefore a European dish into which a product from the Far East is made to fit seamlessly – if the tofu is of good quality, i.e. mild, not very bitter, full-bodied and almost sweet. Then the tofu reminds me of Kyoto, where you can eat it with a spoon like a custard pudding, often accompanied only by soy sauce. This dish came about as a way of showcasing the soya beans and the tofu itself, instead of smothering it with Mediterranean herbs and frying it, because it has greater potential.

Serves 2

15 g hazelnuts
50 g cape gooseberries
*   with papery cape*
2 tbsp sake
½ tsp (1 g) kuzu starch
2 tsp sugar
100 g silken tofu

Dry roast the hazelnuts in a frying pan until golden brown. Put them in a cloth and rub them against each other to loosen the bitter skin as much as possible. It's enough – as usual – if about eighty per cent of it is removed.

Remove the capes from the cape gooseberries and cut them in half. Mix the sake with the kuzu starch. Cook the sugar to a light caramel in a pan. Add the cape gooseberries and toss. Next, stir in the sake kuzu mixture, bring to the boil and remove from the heat.

Cut the tofu into two portions and arrange on two plates. Serve with the candied cape gooseberries and roasted hazelnuts.

CHESTNUT SWEETS

———◇◇◇———

In Japan, I was particularly fascinated by the fine sweets served with tea, known as wagashi. They are small creations made of beans, sugar and often also rice, which capture a particular moment amidst the changing seasons, for instance by giving the sweets the shape of a maple leaf, by encasing them in a thin, clear layer of visually cooling jelly or by wrapping them with a cherry leaf.

These sweets are at their best when they look like the things they are made of, and when the path taken to make them is short and simple.

That's how we came up with these chestnuts. The chestnuts are pressed through a sieve, flavoured only with sugar and salt and then given back their shape. That's all there is to it.

During my 'field research' in Japan, I was in the kitchen of a well-known Kaiseki restaurant in Kyoto as an intern – an honorary title in Japan – and tried my hand at making the exact same shape as on the photo. I spent a long time trying to understand the shape. Without understanding it, I had no chance of success, I thought. In fact – and I believe this also has something to do with Zen – the little balls I liked the best were the ones I made when I wasn't thinking, when my mind was empty and I wasn't being so determined to succeed. Although that doesn't mean I didn't have to practise the shape. So I was all the more pleased that they came out so well again, as I was no longer in Japan, and I was able to give the chestnuts a beautiful and dignified shape.

Serves 2
100 g chestnuts, cooked and peeled
20 g whole-cane sugar (e.g. muscovado sugar)
1 pinch salt

Press the cooked and peeled chestnuts through a sieve. Mix the sugar and salt into the paste, gradually adding 10 ml of water. There is a certain point where the balls hold their shape, but don't yet become wet and heavy. That's what you have to aim for.

Moisten and wring out a cloth napkin. Divide the chestnut mixture into six portions. Place each portion individually in the middle of the napkin. Use your thumb, middle finger and index finger to hold and give the mixture the shape of a small ball with part gently squeezed between your fingers. The result should be a pretty cone-shaped tip. Don't be tense; empty your mind, stay relaxed and practise patiently.

Serve with matcha and enjoy the flavour of the chestnuts and the sense of your own accomplishment.

BARLEY TEA

———◇◇◇———

Mugicha is the name given to barley tea in Japan, which is often drunk with food. It contains no caffeine, yet it is very tasty and is similar in appearance to genmaicha, green tea with toasted rice grains. Both hot and cold mugicha is available in large containers in the cafeteria of a Kyoto university where you can help yourself to it. It's always surprising how refreshing this tea is, especially in the summer heat. In Japan, it is often sold in tea bags, which makes serving easy. However, this doesn't allow you to see how easy it is to prepare this tea – and what you gain when you freshly roast the barley yourself. Because beauty can be achieved with simplicity. In addition to this, another opportunity for you to discover the beauty and essence of cereals is the buckwheat tea we present in winter.

We don't roast the barley in the oven, even if that gives the most uniform results. On the one hand, the amount we use is too small for this; and on the other hand, because it's impossible to work evenly when stirring with a spoon, the result is a wider range of flavours in the grain.

Most importantly of all, you have to be closely involved in the process. The time you take allows you to perceive the changes and you build up anticipation for the pleasure to come.

Serves 2

2 tbsp barley (or 1 tbsp, 10–12 g, per portion)

Dry-roast the barley in a frying pan (if possible with a thick bottom) over a medium heat until its aroma develops and the grains have mild and sweetish flavour and a rich fragrance.

Bring 400 ml of water to the boil, put 1 tablespoon of barley into each teacup, pour over the water and leave to steep for at least 6 minutes.

Tip: You can also make barley tea by cold extraction for hot days: simply pour 200 ml of water over 10–12 g of roasted barley and refrigerate overnight.

For us, however, barley tea is for autumn because there is something sweet and golden about it; it brings back the feeling of summer and it can adapt easily and wonderfully to the changeable weather – at times the warmth of a late summer, and at others the cold and rain of November.

WINTER

What is winter?

It is a time of contrasts – between nature outside and the spaces we create to meet our needs for warmth, light and good company. Aside from warmth and cold, light and dark, inside and outside, it's about solitude and togetherness, finishing up with the old and letting the new begin.

We want to find physical, mental, spiritual and social warmth. Fire plays an important role, and the things we eat are pickled or have been previously stored, or they come from the south. They are mainly roots and tubers, and occasionally leaves such as lamb's lettuce. Interestingly, it's also the season for citrus fruits, which bring juiciness, sweetness and sunshine to the table. And they go well with rich broths and earthy aromas.

Winter is a changeable time, shifting between depressingly overcast skies and bone-chilling damp to crisp and clear, and snow that makes everything soft, white and bright. And the winter is long. You sometimes forget that it can stretch into March and that snow can still fall in April. That's when the foresight you showed last summer and autumn, when everything was still in abundance, proves to be of value. It's the kind of 'reserve' we like to use and really believe in.

KUMQUAT AND PINE NUTS

———◇◇◇———

It was a special moment when the photo of this dish first lit up on the screen in front of us. Because it shows some of the things we believe are important.

'Now, is this dessert?' you might ask. What we say is: it is what it is, and take it as it is – a little something that can be served with tea, but which can also be a course in a meal.

Our inspiration for this dish was something we found in a Japanese cookbook on fermented food, which, contrary to what we had assumed, wasn't only about vegetables and miso. Kumquats, we learnt, are native to Japan and ripen in winter. There they are called kinkan ('golden citrus fruit') and give an idea of the wide variety of citrus fruits in the Far East that we hardly know in our country, such as yuzu and sudachi.

The result is a kind of culinary still life, because although the components are clearly defined by shape and colour, they are tastefully and pleasantly restrained in the Japanese sense. This makes it a good accompaniment for tea. It sets the tone for our winter dishes, and therefore is the starting point for our menu.

Serves 2

80-100 g organic
    kumquats
1½ tbsp dark soy sauce
25 g whole-cane sugar
1 pinch salt
2–3 thin slices of ginger
    (optional)
3 tbsp organic pine nuts

Make cuts lengthways all around the kumquats. Bring 25 ml of water to the boil and add the soy sauce, sugar and salt. Optionally, also add the ginger. Reduce the heat, add the kumquats and cook over a moderate heat according to preference. They lose some of their tartness and hardness. I simmered them for about 5 minutes. They should be poached until soft.

Dry-roast the pine nuts in a frying pan. Leave the kumquats whole or cut them into pieces, according to preference, and serve with the pine nuts and some of the resulting syrup.

BEETROOT SOUP

———◇◇◇———

This soup, made from only two vegetables, is restrained and yet rich and warming. As with the clear soups from the other seasons, the ultimate goal is to bring out the specific flavour of the beetroot with the dashi. Every beetroot is different, so the measures given for salt, sweeteners (sugar, mirin and sake) and chilli pepper are only approximate. It's important that you taste the soup and very carefully adjust the seasoning. Then it will become an elegant dish with something gentle about it, even when the heat from the chilli rises as it is eaten.

Serves 2

125 g beetroot

Sugar

400 ml kombu dashi

2–3 thin slices of ginger

50 g mushrooms (we used shimeji mushrooms, alternatively, use enoki mushrooms)

Oil for frying

1 dash sake

1 pinch salt

2 tsp mirin

1 tsp soy sauce

5–6 slices chilli pepper, mild to medium hot variety

Peel, halve, and cut the beetroot into wedges. Cook 1 teaspoon of sugar to a light caramel in a pan. Deglaze with the dashi, bring to the boil and cook the beetroot in the liquid until firm to the bite. Add the ginger, remove from heat and leave to stand for a short time.

In the meantime, clean the mushrooms. Heat a frying pan, add a little oil and spread it around with kitchen paper. Sauté the mushrooms on one side until nicely coloured. Then turn them over. Deglaze with the sake and gently sprinkle with a few grains of salt. Remove the pan from the heat.

Season the soup with mirin, soy sauce, salt and possibly sugar to give it a balanced and mild taste. Add the chilli. Serve in bowls with the mushrooms.

CELERIAC ESCALOPE

———◇◇◇———

Sometimes you think you've seen it all and that your own achievements are the best. Panko is something that suddenly frustrates this way of thinking. As legendary as tempura seems to us in Europe, the Japanese way of using breadcrumbs is equally beautiful. Panko is a neologism made up of the word *pan*, meaning 'bread', and *ko*, the word for 'flour'. The crumbs are light in colour with a distinct taste and have a clean, irregular size, which makes them crunchy and forms a thick coating.

We combine panko with the first vegetarian dish I became familiar with at the school where I trained as a cook, celeriac escalope, which I still love today.

This is a very easy way of making celeriac escalope: you just coat it with breadcrumbs, bake it and eat it while still hot dipped in a little salt. This is one of the nicest ways to enjoy celeriac.

Serves 2

1 (about 100-g) celeriac, peeled
100 g flour
1 tsp mirin
1 tsp soy sauce
1 pinch salt
100 g panko
Oil for deep-frying
Salt flakes for serving

Slice the celeriac. You can decide how thick you want the slices yourself. I like thin slices, 3–5 mm thick.

Gradually mix about 140 ml of water into the flour to make a thick and sticky batter. Stir in the mirin, soy sauce and salt. Dip the celeriac slices in the batter and then in the panko.

Heat about 2 cm of oil in a small frying pan over a medium heat and fry the celeriac slices on both sides until golden brown. Drain briefly on kitchen paper or in a sieve. Sprinkle with a few salt flakes and serve.

Tip: Celeriac escalope goes well with the misonnaise shown on page 128.

LEEK, ORANGE AND WALNUT

———◇◇◇———

This is a simple dish that brings together three things that are available almost all year round. Because leeks are still grown in the fields in winter, people start cracking walnuts around Christmas and citrus fruits are at their peak flavour in the dark season, now is a good time to combine them practically on their own in a quick dish. The orange brings freshness, juiciness and sun to everything. The honey coats and binds the ingredients, just as a good sauce usually does in European dishes.

Serves 2

100–120 g leek
1 tsp honey
½ tsp sangohachi,
*   alternatively 1 tsp*
*   mild-flavoured light*
*   soy sauce*
1 orange slice, about 2
*   cm thick, cut from the*
*   middle*
2 tbsp (20–30-g) shelled
*   walnuts*
Oil for frying

Cut the leek into about 1½-cm-thick strips. Marinate with the honey and sangohachi for 5 minutes.

Remove the peel from the orange slice and divide into segments.

Dry-roast the walnuts in a small frying pan. If necessary, rub them against each other in a cloth to remove their skins.

Oil the frying pan and raise the heat to high. Take the leek strips out of the marinade and wipe off some of the excess. Sear the leeks briefly in the frying pan.

Put the walnuts and orange pieces into the marinade and coat. Arrange the leek, walnuts and orange pieces separately in a bowl and serve.

PARSNIP, SESAME AND CHILLI

———◇◇◇———

Parsnips are one of those vegetables that are easily underestimated because they have a somewhat woody and crumbly texture and insipid taste that we don't find appealing. Which is why we don't really know them at all. So we were all the more surprised at how quickly and easily you can coax out their beauty and flavour with just a few seasoning ingredients, a frying pan and a knife. But a word of warning: here we see what it means when we say cooking is cutting. The thicker you cut the parsnip sticks, the more they become floury and crumbly. We also say: fine is fine. In other words, cut into fine batons, about the width of a chopstick, they taste just fine.

Serves 2

120–140 g parsnips
1 tsp sugar
1 tbsp neutral vegetable oil
1 tsp light soy sauce
1 tbsp mirin
5–6 small slices of chilli
    pepper
1 tsp toasted sesame seeds
Salt

Organic parsnips don't need peeling; just brush their skin well. This keeps in more of their flavour. Cut the parsnip lengthwise into batons.

Heat a frying pan and cook the sugar to a light caramel. Add the parsnips and toss. Then add the oil and fry the parsnip batons until golden brown. In a heavy pan over a high heat, this should take 2–3 minutes.

Remove the pan from the heat and stir in the soy sauce, mirin, chilli and sesame seeds. Season with salt. Cover with a lid and cook for 1 minute. Then serve.

A dish that warms and makes you feel good.

FLAKED ALMOND TOFU

––––◇◇––––

A little over a year ago I ate a meal prepared by Mari Fujii, the widow of a Zen monastery cook. She's continuing the work of her late husband to preserve and familiarise people with Shojin Ryori, the festive cuisine of Zen monasteries. The food Mari prepared was quite an experience, and it was very inspiring because it showed how Japanese and local produce can be combined with simple seasoning ingredients to create a light, colourful and harmonious meal. And it showed how to cook with the heart. She gave me a cookbook which contained this beautiful flaked almond tofu.

I tried it out for our cookbook and then thought for a long time about how it could be changed or adapted. But I came to the conclusion that there was nothing lacking. I find it so coherent and complete. The only thing I left out of the recipe was lemon and lemon juice. And so I would like to pass on the lesson I learnt: cooking with the heart is the most important ingredient!

The dish is restrained and only lightly spiced. It is easy to prepare and, on the whole, simple in the best sense of the word. If you pay close attention, you can discern the sweet, roasted taste of the almonds and their summer ripeness. And the juicy softness of soya beans curdled to make the tofu. It has both dignity and depth, just like the cook Mari Fujii who delighted me with her food at the time.

Serves 2
100 g firm tofu
30 g flour
40 g flaked almonds
Oil for frying
Salt flakes for serving

Cut the tofu into three or four pieces of equal size. Pat carefully with kitchen paper to absorb some of the moisture.

Mix the flour with 50 ml of water to make a batter with the consistency of pancake batter. Dip the tofu in the batter and then roll in the flaked almonds. Set aside on a plate.

Heat some oil in a small frying pan or saucepan (about 1½ cm deep) over a medium heat. Fry the almond-coated tofu pieces until golden brown on all sides. Drain on kitchen paper and sprinkle with salt flakes. Serve hot.

SAVOY CABBAGE AND HAZELNUTS

—◇◇◇—

Do they have Savoy cabbage in Japan? I never saw any when I was there. Even hazelnuts can only be found in very small packages on the shelves of large Japanese supermarkets sold with ingredients to make European-style cakes and tarts.

But if they did have Savoy cabbage there, what would the Japanese do with it? Perhaps they'd do the same thing we have in mind, which is Savoy cabbage as Savoy cabbage.

Savoy cabbage is a splendid cabbage variety, with a very distinct, aesthetically pleasing leaf structure and with very different taste profiles between the outermost leaf and the heart, especially when gently cooked. It also has a wonderfully nutty taste, which is enhanced by the hazelnuts. It benefited from a little acidity, so we added the lemon zest. Otherwise it is seasoned as usual with sake, mirin and soy sauce. As a result, its flavour reflects what it is.

Serves 2

2 tbsp hazelnuts

100 g Savoy cabbage (3–4 leaves, depending on size)

2–3 tbsp oil

1 strip zest from an untreated lemon

3 tbsp sake

1 tbsp mirin

1 tsp light soy sauce

Dry-roast the nuts in a frying pan over a moderate heat, tilting the pan from time to time. Then coarsely crush the nuts in a mortar.

Clean the cabbage leaves. Depending on preference, use a combination of the outermost and innermost leaves, or only those from the centre. The outer leaves take longer to cook and should be added to the pan earlier. Cut the leaves into diamond shapes 1½–2 cm in width.

Heat the oil in a pan and quickly sauté the cabbage together with the hazelnuts and lemon zest. Mix 50 ml of water with the sake, mirin and light soy sauce and add to the pan. Cover with a lid on and cook for 5–8 minutes over a moderate heat. Transfer the cabbage to a container and reduce the remaining cooking liquid to 2 tablespoons. NB: Depending on the pan and stove, the liquid may already have evaporated by the time the cabbage is cooked. If you hear a crackling or frying sound, make sure you add water. If this is not the case, reduce the liquid to 2 tablespoons as described.

Mix the cabbage well with the resulting sauce and serve.

DAIKON, MANDARIN AND TOFU

Daikon – the large, white and mild-flavoured Japanese radish – is one of the most important vegetables in Japan. In winter, it is simmered for hours together with eggs, fish paste or deep-fried tofu pockets to make a steaming stew called oden. Now soaked like a sponge, the daikon tastes like the rich stock in which it was cooked, and gives off a lovely warmth.

Kiriboshi daikon are the dried daikon strips that last for ages, especially over the winter. They also have a strong smell. They come back to life when soaked in water. And like the shimmering daikon in oden, they're able to absorb liquids and go well with soy sauce and sweetness. The latter is provided by the mandarin, a very popular winter fruit. By the way, the Japan mandarin is the mikan. The closest equivalent in this country is satsuma.

The tofu acts in a similar way to the soaked daikon. It is lightly dusted with flour and then fried in about 4 cm of oil. The oil is good for it. Its pores open easily and it becomes fluffy, enabling it to absorb liquid.

A little paprika adds dimension to the dish, both in terms of colour and aroma, without going too far.

The result is a wintry trio of radish, tofu and mandarin with a hint of paprika.

Serves 2

15 g kiriboshi daikon (dried daikon, available in Asian or Oriental shops or online)

4 tbsp kombu dashi

1 tbsp sake

1 tbsp mirin

1 tsp light soy sauce

1 pinch salt

1 mandarin

1–2 pinches of sugar, according to preference

Oil for frying

100 g tofu

2 tbsp flour

2 pinches paprika powder, sweet or hot according to preference

Soak the dried daikon strips in 200 ml of water for 30 minutes.

Next, transfer the daikon to a sieve, collect the soaking water and mix it with the dashi, sake, mirin, soy sauce and salt in a pan and bring to the boil. Add the daikon, cover immediately with a lid the diameter of which is a little smaller than that of the pan and simmer for 5 minutes. As a result, the liquid boils down and the daikon cooks and absorbs the stock.

Peel the mandarin and cut the individual segments in half across the middle.

Remove the lid from the pan and boil down the remaining liquid while gently stirring the daikon. Add the mandarin pieces, cook for a few seconds and gently mix in. Remove the pan from the heat and leave to cool. Taste the daikon and adjust the flavour if necessary with a little sugar.

Heat about 4 cm of oil in a small frying pan. Lightly press the tofu between two sheets of kitchen paper to remove the excess water. Pat dry and dust with the flour. Fry in the hot oil over a medium heat until golden brown on all sides. Drain on kitchen paper or in a sieve and then sprinkle with paprika. Serve with the daikon and mandarin.

METHOD FOR MAKING TEMPURA

Tempura is the Japanese art of deep-frying. The technique was actually introduced to Japan in the sixteenth century by the southern European seafarers – probably Portuguese – as was the name. But in the typical Japanese way, every single detail of the technique has been perfected, with the result that as we sit at the counter of a restaurant specialising exclusively in tempura (sometimes Michelin-starred), it becomes clear to us that there really is an art to it.

Tempura is very popular and is served in many restaurants in all categories. But to understand tempura, it's best to go to one that specialises in it. Across the counter you may see the large copper pot in which the oil is kept hot. It has a considerable diameter, so that when the tempura chef quickly and skilfully slides the food into the oil, it won't influence the temperature and any fluctuations are avoided, because the temperature should always be around 180°C/356°F. It mustn't fall below 170°C/340°F or the batter will absorb too much oil. If this were to happen, it would undo the subtle contradiction the cook is working to create: deep-frying something without it becoming greasy. The essence of tempura is its airiness and lightness.

As if to prove it, the finished tempura is served on white paper, so that you can see with your own eyes that there are hardly any oily stains. That's the way it should be. The batter just forms a crispy, light shell under which the flavour of the food can concentrate. Tempura is all about purity and – as is often the case in Japan – paring things down to the essentials.

For our tempura batter we use:
90 g organic flour (type 550 or plain flour because it's more substantial)
140 ml ice-cold water (for a thinner batter, e.g. for kale, use 60 g flour and 100 ml ice-cold water)

The batter typically contains only water, flour and egg. One might think that there's little room for manoeuvre and that everything is actually already predetermined. However – and this is another insight that I have gained time and again in Japan – it is precisely the intensive use of three ingredients that provides scope for a wide range of variations. Some people mix the flour with starch or use rice flour, whereas others say that normal wheat flour is the best. Some people use normal tap water, while others believe it should be filtered and others are adamant that it should be carbonated, or even mixed with white wine or vodka. Nevertheless, what everyone does agree on is that it must be ice cold.

Some people use whole eggs and others only yolks. Egg is omitted from the vegan cuisine of Zen temples and monasteries and the batter consists only of water and flour. This is also the path we've taken. We wanted to start with the essentials in order to understand the basic idea. The resulting batter becomes a little firmer, but the result is good. It was also important for us to show how few ingredients are really needed – and that you don't really need egg to make tempura.

Every flour behaves differently, so your own judgement is crucial. For fine leaves such as carrot tops and celery and kale leaves, the batter should be a little thinner, and it should be a little thicker and firmer for carrot or rhubarb.

Technique is critical for tempura. As I said, the water should be ice cold. As previously explained in the corresponding recipes, a bowl is lined with ice packs and filled with water. We put the bowl for the batter inside this ice bath. There must be no mad rush at the stove. Hot oil needs close attention. This isn't only because the temperature should be precise, but also because it can quickly become dangerous.

The batter is made in a way that people might find unusual: the flour and water are mixed only lightly and briefly using chopsticks, and any lumps forming during the process are intentional. Too much mixing activates the gluten in the flour and makes the batter heavy. At least that's one explanation.

The vegetables are first dusted with flour, tapped to remove the excess and then dipped in the batter. Next, they're slid into the oil in small batches and cooked until the bubbles in the oil become smaller and the bubbling dies down.

You don't sit right at the counter of a tempura restaurant for nothing. The precise movements made by the chef become part of the tasting experience, giving an idea of the goodness that is about to emerge from the oil. What's more, tempura should be eaten very quickly after cooking because that's when it's at its best. Its quality declines very quickly as it cools. So don't wait too long. The dipping sauce should be ready beforehand. Otherwise, just a few salt flakes will suffice. Some people also like a splash of lemon juice with theirs.

Contrary to our experience with chip stalls in this country, no smell of grease sticks to your clothes when leaving a tempura restaurant. This may because of the powerful but quiet extractor fans. And the freshness of the oil. If you make tempura yourself, don't reuse the oil. And regularly strain it through a sieve into a metal bowl or another pan after frying each batch to remove the bits of batter that settle at the bottom as these increasingly affect the smell and taste of the oil. Wipe the empty pan dry with kitchen paper (never clean with water as any left in the pan can cause the oil to splatter a lot), then put the filtered oil back into the pan and continue.

Incidentally, farmers in Kyoto are the grateful recipients of the oil used by the tempura chefs. They use it to fertilize their vegetables, which may later be served again under a fine coating of batter, in an endless cycle of growing and eating vegetables at their peak. As I said, it isn't about the crispy batter, but about what's underneath. About the nature of things.

KALE TEMPURA

———◇◇◇———

Sometimes it takes a detour through another culture to rediscover the value of everyday things. This is also true of kale, which for a long time we were only familiar with in a stew cooked for hours and eaten in winter with ribs or sausage and potatoes, and whose heaviness was especially beneficial for the nap taken after this meal.

And then it suddenly came back to us a few years ago, mainly in the form of 'kale chips'.

We came up with the idea of crispy kale fritters, but sent the leafy vegetables via Japan to be encased in tempura. There is something light and mysterious about it, because the batter covers the leaf and yet showcases its wild and feathery structure. Deep-frying takes away some of its heaviness. NB: The stalks are somewhat tough, so you score them several times from side to side before battering.

Serves 2
Oil for deep-frying
60 g flour (e.g. type 550,
*   plain flour) plus more*
*   for dusting*
90–120 g kale leaves
2–3 pinches salt flakes

Heat the oil in a pan or deep-fryer to 180°C/356°F.

Make tempura batter with the flour and 100 ml of ice-cold water according to the recipe on page 178; it should be relatively thin.

Dust the kale leaves with flour and tap off the excess. Dip the leaves in the batter, allowing a little to run off. Fry in the oil until the bubbles in the oil become smaller and the bubbling dies down. Drain in a sieve or on kitchen paper.

Serve hot. Sprinkle with salt flakes or dip into the salt flakes, according to preference.

WINTER SQUASH, PUMPKIN SEEDS AND MANDARIN

Is winter squash actually a winter vegetable or does it belong to autumn? Fewer and fewer varieties are available at this dark time of year until only the Uchiki Kuri squash, also known as Red Kuri, Orange Hokkaido or Japanese red onion squash, remains. But this brightly coloured squash brings summer and autumn back to the table. Provided we can find it, Kabocha squash, also known as Green Hokkaido squash, is always our first choice. Unfortunately, it's quite rare. But seeing as Jule had planted it, it came straight from the garden and into our cookbook.

When it comes to eating winter squash as winter squash, the special thing about this variety is its crumbly texture. Other varieties are firmer and crunchier or they have long fibres and a flavour similar to that of a cucumber. Kabocha squash is very popular in Japan, where it's used for confectionery, among other things, or prepared in the simplest way: cooked cleanly and seasoned with soy sauce and the like.

There are two more special features in the preparation of this squash. The first is that, in Japanese cuisine, the edges of each piece of the squash are rounded off by running a knife around it. And the second, which fascinates me even more, is that the skin is partially peeled with a knife, so that a strange, aesthetically pleasing pattern appears and the orange flesh shines through. Aesthetics is also taste: not only does the squash look nicer, but it is also easier to eat because the skin does not completely cover the outside of the pieces. At the same time, the contrast between the skin and the flesh is increased, so that the different aspects of the squash can be perceived more clearly in a small bite. It's very Japanese to bring the best out of the smallest of things with the existing possibilities, and to serve them in the greatest simplicity.

WINTER SQUASH, PUMPKIN SEEDS AND MANDARIN

—◇◇◇—

Serves 2

200–250 g winter squash
  (preferably Kabocha
  squash)
1 tsp sugar
1 pinch salt
2 tbsp pumpkin seeds
1 tsp mandarin
  marmalade
1–2 drops vinegar

Cut the squash into wedges and, according to preference, cut the wedges into smaller pieces. Use a knife to round off the sharp edges. Also peel the skin thinly with a knife in different places, so that the underlying layer or the flesh of the fruit shows through.

Bring 200 ml of water to the boil in a pan and add the sugar and salt. Put the squash into the pan to cook. It's best to cover the squash directly with a lid the diameter of which is a little smaller than that of the pan. This allows the liquid at the sides to evaporate and the squash to cook under the lid. Quickly lift the lid and turn the squash from time to time.

In the meantime, gently dry-roast the pumpkin seeds in a frying pan. Then chop them roughly and mix with the marmalade and add a few drops (literally only drops!) of vinegar. Even such a small amount is enough to remove sweetness from the sauce and ensure that it blends in well with the squash.

When the squash is cooked, take it out and leave it to rest for a little while. If there is still cooking liquid in the pan, reduce it down, return the squash to the pan and coat well.

Serve the squash and the sauce separately, according to preference, or gently mix them together shortly before serving. Plate the dish with kindness and serenity because, as I said previously, aesthetics is taste, and vice versa.

RADICCHIO, APPLE AND BUCKWHEAT FURIKAKE

—◇◇◇—

Furikake is the name given in Japan to all the things that are sprinkled over rice. It comes in a large variety of ready-to-use mixes, mostly containing nori seaweed and bonito flakes, and sometimes also with dried egg yolk and other seasonings. It's rare not to find monosodium glutamate, which is added to almost any ready-made products in Japan that aren't sweet.

The alternative is to make it yourself. And there's an infinite range of things that can be roasted and dried in a frying pan.

If you have buckwheat grains to spare, for instance, after making buckwheat tea, they're ideal for this. We sprinkle them over Radicchio Rosso di Treviso, one of the most beautiful salad vegetables I know. It has such a wonderful colour, the structure of the leaves is so aesthetically pleasing that I rarely dare to cut them up, and it has a delicately bitter flavour. The radicchio here combines beautifully with apple, which adds a little softness, sweetness and whimsy, and also with the buckwheat, which adds nuttiness, substance and crunch.

Radicchio is a winter vegetable, by the way. At least it's available fresh south of the Alps, in Italy.

Serves 2

3 tbsp buckwheat
2 tbsp mirin
4 tbsp sake
1 tbsp soy sauce
Sugar
1 medium (about 120-g) apple
1–2 tsp rice vinegar
3–4 tsp neutral oil
Salt
1 (100–120-g) head Radicchio Rosso di Treviso, alternatively normal radicchio or chicory

Dry-roast the buckwheat in a heavy frying pan over a medium heat, stirring occasionally. Reduce the heat at the end. Add 1 tablespoon of mirin, 2 tablespoons of sake, the soy sauce and 2 pinches of sugar and toss the buckwheat in the liquid until it boils away and the grains are well-coated.

Core the apple without peeling and cut into about 1-cm dice. Cook half a teaspoon of sugar to a light caramel in a small saucepan. Add the diced apple, 2 tablespoons of sake and 1 tablespoon of mirin. Cover with a lid and cook the apple over a low heat. This can take up to 10 minutes. There should still be 1–2 tablespoons of liquid left in the pan. Otherwise, add some water to the pan and stir once. Collect the cooking liquid and mix with the vinegar and oil to make a dressing. Season with salt.

Divide the radicchio into individual leaves and put them into a large bowl. Add the apple cubes and dressing. Use your hands to gently mix everything together. Arrange on a plate, sprinkle with the buckwheat grains and serve.

KIND OF KIMCHI
RED CABBAGE AND CHINESE CABBAGE

Kimchi is also very popular in Japan. Chinese cabbage kimchi is quick to prepare and is perfect for the winter. In this version, Chinese cabbage, known as hakusai in Japanese, forms an interesting East-West connection with red cabbage. The base is provided by the sugar and garlic, enhanced by the kombu, which come together in a fascinating way similar to that of sugar and soy sauce.

Red cabbage, with which we are familiar in the braised pickled red cabbage dish, needs the addition of a lot of sweetness and moisture, otherwise it gives the impression of being insipid and unrefined. It works better if it's shredded or sliced as thinly as possible after fermenting. Red cabbage takes longer to develop its flavour than Chinese cabbage.

Serves 2

For the Chinese cabbage

About 250 g Chinese cabbage

4 tsp sugar

2 per cent salt (based on the weight of the cabbage after cleaning)

2 cloves garlic

10 g fresh ginger

3–4 g chilli powder

½ tsp soy sauce

1 finger-length piece of kombu, about 1½ cm wide

For the red cabbage

160 g red cabbage

4 tsp sugar

2 per cent salt (based on the weight of the cabbage after cleaning)

The weight measures given in the recipe equate to about half a small head of Chinese cabbage and a quarter of a head of red cabbage. It's important to leave the leaves attached to the stem. They need to be opened out when they're spread all over with their respective paste.

To make the paste, the ingredients listed are ground together in a mortar, except the kombu. It's good to start with the grainy ingredients first, in other words the sugar and salt, as well as the garlic because it's held by the grains and is easily ground down.

Then spread the respective paste over the individual leaves of the two types of cabbage and massage it in. The sugar and salt release the water in the leaves and a brine forms. I then put the cabbage leaves in a resealable bag, add the kombu and squeeze the air out before sealing the bags and putting a weight on them, such as a stone. Because of the brine that's formed, the Chinese cabbage and red cabbage can be left to ferment outside the refrigerator. At the beginning it's important to check them once a day and to squeeze the air out frequently.

Although conditions differ in every kitchen and in every season, the Chinese cabbage will probably be ready after just one day. Red cabbage tends to take three to four days or more. In this case, you have to use your senses, check the state of development and judge according to preference.

The Chinese cabbage becomes wonderfully soft and can be served in large pieces. Slice the red cabbage as thinly as possible, as mentioned above.

5 g fresh ginger
5 g fresh horseradish
1 finger-length strip of
    untreated lemon zest,
    about 1½ cm wide
1 finger-length piece of
    kombu, about 1½ cm
    wide

MISO SOUP, WINTER VEGETABLES AND SESAME TOFU

Miso soup is a soup to have every day. It's an essential part of the traditional Japanese breakfast and is served with a bowl of rice and pickled vegetables. It's often served in hotels on a tray with a slice of grilled salmon. The different types of dashi are mostly available in the form of instant powders and granules in sachets. Together with an excellent miso paste, the other basic ingredient is water. It's quick and simple.

The nice thing about miso soup in the morning is that it warms the stomach wonderfully. Buttered bread, on the other hand, has to come to the right temperature in the stomach first, and just for that to happen you need more energy, which actually comes from eating. With miso soup for breakfast, you're already warmed up to face the cold of winter, which they also have in Japan.

We were guided by this idea, although the dashi we use is home-made. The accompanying vegetables can be chosen freely according to availability, such as carrots, parsnips, leeks and celeriac. These all keep over the winter and are always available.

As is common in Japan, the intensity of the stocks, broths and soups increases in winter, and people like to use more robust miso pastes. We've taken note of this and use a miso paste made with whole soya beans and brown rice.

Tofu is also added to the soup as a classic garnish. However, here it's quickly and easily coated in sesame seeds and briefly fried in oil until golden brown. We don't add salt to the tofu, because, protected by the sesame seeds, it forms a soft and clear void in the richly flavoured miso soup.

Fortified in this way, we can face the cold and dark winter days.

Serves 2
80–100 g tofu
1 tbsp plain flour
3 tbsp sesame seeds
Oil for frying
150 g vegetables, e.g.
    carrot, celeriac, leek,
    parsnip
400 ml kombu dashi
3–4 tsp mirin
40 g miso paste
Salt

Cut the tofu into cubes (at least the size of your thumb tip, about 3 cm). Make a batter by mixing the flour with 2 tablespoons of water. Dip the tofu in the batter and roll in the sesame seeds. Set aside on kitchen paper.

Heat about 2 cm of oil in a small frying pan. Fry the tofu cubes on two opposing sides over a medium heat until golden brown (the remaining sides should also turn golden in the process).

Cut the vegetables into batons. Heat the dashi and add the mirin. Cook the vegetable sticks in the dashi, leaving them firm to the bite. Reduce the heat and stir in the miso paste. The soup needs no further cooking. Season with salt.

Serve the soup with the vegetable batons and tofu cubes.

VEGETABLE RICE

— ◇◆◇ —

In winter, the flavour of soups, stocks and broths in Japanese cuisine become deeper and richer. They're meant to warm both the body and the soul. Again, the base is formed by combining the sweetness of mirin and sugar with soy sauce.

Additional sweetness is also provided by the vegetables cooked directly with the rice. Prepared this way, the rice isn't unseasoned and white, but a warm and cosy, caramel brown. My favourite recipe for dark, freezing-cold winter evenings in Kyoto.

Serves 2

4 small dried shiitake
mushrooms
1 g kombu kelp
140 g rice
About 50 g parsnip
About 30 g celeriac
About 30 g carrot
5 g fresh ginger
1 tbsp soy sauce
2 tbsp mirin
2 pinches salt
1 pinch of sugar
if required

To make the stock, bring 200 ml of water to the boil and soak the mushrooms in it. When the liquid has cooled down slightly, add the kombu.

Wash the rice thoroughly according to the recipe on page 56, drain and rest for 30 minutes.

In the meantime, cut the vegetables lengthways into thin strips. Slice the ginger and then cut into strips.

Take the mushrooms out of the stock and cut into slices. Weigh the rice and add 110 per cent of its weight in stock. Add the vegetable and ginger strips, mushrooms, soy sauce, mirin and salt, and the sugar if required. Keep the kombu in the stock. Cook everything together in a pan according to the basic rice recipe. NB: This vegetable rice burns more easily than unseasoned white rice, so pay close attention to sounds and smells.

Serve hot. This rice also tastes good the next day.

RED BEAN RICE

⸻◇◇◇⸻

It took us a long time to decide whether to include a recipe for red bean rice. This dish has great cultural and symbolic significance in Japan and is served on different festive occasions, most likely as a reminder of the red rice that was once served as an offering to kami, Shinto deities, many centuries ago. The Japanese name for this red rice is sekihan and the dish is actually prepared using glutinous rice. However, we've decided to use normal round or short-grain rice.

Actually, you only need a very small amount of beans for this rice. It also makes little sense to only boil two or three tablespoons of beans. We ended up including the recipe anyway, convinced by its flavour and visual beauty. Perhaps you can use a few leftover azuki beans from another recipe; alternatively, you can cook a larger quantity of beans and make anko with the remainder (see page 65). You also come to appreciate the little things and to know that taking a more tortuous path often has its reward.

Serves 2
2–3 tbsp azuki beans
140 g rice
1 tbsp sake
½ tsp sugar
1 pinch salt
1 tsp toasted black
*   sesame seeds*

Prepare the beans according to the instructions on the packet, i.e. soak them overnight and then cook until firm to the bite (they shouldn't be too soft because they're also going to cook with the rice).

While the beans are cooking, wash the rice as described in the basic recipe on page 56, leave to rest and add 110 per cent of the weight of the rested rice in water. Add the sake, sugar, salt and the cooked beans. Cook according to the basic recipe: bring to the boil in the covered pan over a medium heat, reduce the heat right down and continue to cook until all the water is absorbed and you hear a crackling sound. Remove the pan from the heat. Take off the lid, wipe the edges, cover the pan again and let the rice rest for at least 15 minutes.

Serve sprinkled with the toasted black sesame seeds.

SWEET POTATO WITH SESAME SEEDS

––––––◇◇◇––––––

When you walk through the narrow streets of Kyoto's old town, you can sometimes smell sweet potatoes cooking and slowly caramelising over a fire or on hot stones. Their sweetness then becomes very noticeable. The line between sweet and savoury in Japan is less defined. For instance, sweet potatoes are used as an ingredient in traditional sweets.

There are said to be over a hundred different varieties of sweet potatoes in Japan, ranging in colour from light yellow and golden to purple. Their flavour is sometimes milder and sometimes sweeter. So there is plenty of choice for the most diverse uses.

We've taken up this idea of the interplay between sweet and savoury. Is this dish a dessert, or does the sweet potato belong to the realm of vegetables and savoury foods? Not only but also. We can well imagine them as a sweet to accompany sencha in the afternoon. Or kale tempura, beetroot soup and rice.

Actually, we think things are what they are, which means there are no categories of sweet and savoury.

Serves 2

1 (120–150-g) piece sweet
   potato
2 tsp sugar
2 tbsp sake
1 tsp light soy sauce
2 (about 5 g) thin slices of
   ginger
1 tsp toasted black sesame
   seeds

Cut the sweet potato into pieces of about 4 x 4 cm. If possible, choose a pan with a size that allows the sweet potato pieces to fit side by side on the bottom. Cook the sugar to a light caramel and deglaze with sake. Add the sweet potato pieces and water to cover the pieces halfway. Add the soy sauce and ginger.

In Japanese cuisine, lids are often used that are slightly smaller than the pan, in other words they more or less cover the surface of the bottom while still allowing liquid to evaporate at the edges. This allows cooking to take place while reducing any liquids. Choose a lid that roughly fulfils this function. Otherwise use the lid that fits the pan to cook the sweet potato. Cook over a medium heat until soft. This should take 10–12 minutes. Turn the pieces over halfway through.

If there is still liquid in the pan, take out the potatoes and reduce to an almost syrupy consistency. Return the sweet potato to the pan and coat with the sauce. Sprinkle with toasted black sesame seeds and serve.

Tip: The aim is for the sweet potato to be as crumbly as possible, with a consistency similar to that of marzipan.

QUINCE JELLY AND ELDERBERRY JELLY

<hr/>

We were very lucky that at the end of September fragrant quinces were hanging from the tree and Jule quickly put the steam juicer on the stove. A short time later she had filled it with clear, light pink quince juice and set it down for me next to the chopping board.

I was thinking about a dessert made out of quinces, preferably for the winter, and asked Jule for some elderberry juice, which she had also bottled a few weeks before. I don't know what it was, but tasting the two fruit jellies warmed our hearts, and we knew we had found a suitable ending for our winter menu.

There is a very special tradition surrounding these sorts of jellies in Japan. They are sold in boutiques in beautiful packaging and come in different flavours, such as matcha or azuki bean, and are, as you can probably guess, a very refined and expensive delicacy. So, it's all the better when you have bottled the ingredients yourself at home, because these jellies are prepared in no time at all.

Serves 2

For the quince jelly
120 ml quince juice
1 g agar-agar
1 pinch kuzu starch
1 pinch salt
1 tsp honey
½ tsp sugar

For the elderberry jelly
120 ml elderberry juice
1 g agar-agar
1 pinch kuzu starch
1 pinch salt
1 tsp honey
½ tsp sugar

For the quince jelly, combine all the ingredients in a small saucepan. Bring to the boil and continue to cook for 2–3 more minutes, stirring constantly. Pour into a small rectangular container (e.g. an empty 250-g capacity tub) to a depth of about 2 cm. Leave to set in the refrigerator (this can take 1–3 hours, depending on the pectin content of the fruit).

Repeat the process for the elderberry jelly.

Cut the firm jellies into strips and serve one of each variety on a plate.

Tip: If the jelly does not set properly, add some more agar-agar (up to 1 g), bring to the boil, fill the container and leave to set.

The kuzu starch makes the jelly a little softer.

BUCKWHEAT TEA

—◇◇◇—

Buckwheat is an excellent grain. We already introduced you to it in summer in the form of soba noodles. Buckwheat is particularly easy to digest for diabetics, as it has lower impact on the body's blood sugar than wheat flour when absorbed into the body.

Besides having a cooling effect, buckwheat can also warm. And that's a good quality to have in the places where it thrives, particularly as it can also be grown in colder regions, such as in the mountains around Nagano in Japan. Buckwheat is also part of the food culture of Russia and northern France, where it is made into blinis and buckwheat pancakes known as galettes.

Sobacha, Japanese buckwheat tea, is seldom available in Europe, so we decided to make it ourselves. It's easy and quick to make, and not only is the result very convincing, but it also opens the door to teas made from cereals.

Serves 2
2 tbsp buckwheat

The taste can be determined by the degree of toasting. For tea with a mild and rounded flavour, toast the buckwheat in a frying pan over a medium heat, stirring occasionally. Covering the pan with a lid distributes the heat more efficiently and the grains toast more evenly. If you like a more complex flavour, put the grain into a very hot frying pan and brown well, and then quickly remove it from the heat. This allows the toasted aromas from the dark parts of the grain to mix with the mild flavour of the untoasted parts.

Then bring 400 ml of water to the boil. Put 1 tablespoon of toasted buckwheat grains into each teacup, pour over the water and steep for at least 2 minutes and as long as 10 minutes. Put your nose to the cup and breathe in deeply; there's a wonderful simplicity to be found inside it. Enjoy the tea hot, although it tastes good cold too.

If you don't want to eat the grains with the tea, you can take them out and enjoy them later mixed into a salad or steamed rice.

GLOSSARY

Anko: see page 65

Dashi: The vegan version of the famous basic stock of Japanese cuisine uses only kombu or kombu and dried shiitake mushrooms. The traditional version is a combination of kombu and smoked bonito flakes. This stock effectively and almost imperceptibly enhances the flavour inherent to the food.

Edamame: see page 26

Kiriboshi daikon: see page 177

Kombu: Kombu kelp is a type of seaweed that plays an important part in Japanese cuisine on the whole and Zen temple cuisine in particular. It is mainly used to make dashi stock and wherever the intrinsic flavour of ingredients is meant to be accentuated in a light and restrained way. Kombu is also available as tsukudani, a liquorice-like snack; oboro kombu, thinly scraped salty threads; and kombucha, kombu tea.

Kuromitsu: Literally meaning 'black honey', this is a dark, rich and highly aromatic syrup made from unrefined cane sugar. In Japan there's a large variety of very fine sugars, such as the famous wasanbon and the black sugar known as kurozato. Kuromitsu is easy to make yourself, for example using a whole-cane sugar like Muscovado.

Kuzu (also kudzu): A thickening agent, kuzu starch, is obtained from the root tubers of this climbing plant *(Pueraria lobata)*. It is tasteless, sets clear and has a fine consistency compared to potato starch. It is particularly used to make gomadofu (sesame tofu) and noodles (somen).

Mirin: This almost liqueur-like sweet wine, which is made from rice shochu (brandy) and glutinous rice with the help of koji mould, is indispensable in Japanese cuisine. It has a rounded taste and adds a delicate sweetness, shine and body to dishes. It is important to use a quality product. Simple versions contain sugar syrup, while the best quality mirins (hon mirin) are artisanally made and are quite dry and reminiscent of sherry.

Miso: This seasoning paste is rich in umami. It's mostly made from soya beans and rice fermented with koji mould. The varieties range from light and sweetish to almost black, liquorice-like and sour. Choose unpasteurised miso paste that doesn't contain any alcohol or artificial additives, preferably organic.

Mugi (barley): see page 159

Panko: These Japanese breadcrumbs are more like lightly coloured flakes than the finer crumbs we have in this country. Panko has a clean taste and results in a fine and airy crumb coating.

Ponzu: Ponzu actually refers to the juice of citrus fruits such as lemon or sudachi. However, the word is now commonly used for the dipping sauce made with citrus juice and soy sauce.

Sake: The famous rice wine is fermented with koji mould. It has a slightly yeasty and full-bodied, yet restrained flavour. Sake is indispensable in Japanese cuisine and adds complexity and finesse to dishes.

Sangohachi: Is a paste made from rice fermented with salt and koji mould. It isn't very well known, even in Japan. It provides a clean and distinct form of umami flavour like that of miso or soy sauce.

Shiitake mushroom: This is one of the most important mushrooms used in Japanese cuisine. When dried, it develops flavour-enhancing properties and is used in Zen temple cuisine together with kombu to make vegan dashi.

Shiso (perilla): This slightly minty-flavoured green or purple leaf is now also more readily found in our part of the world, but it lacks the characteristic strong resinous aroma. The flowers also have a delicate flavour. The purply red leaves give Japanese pickles (shibatsuke) or umeboshi (salted Japanese plums) their special colour. Shiso tempura is a classic dish.

Soba (buckwheat): see pages 61, 201

Soya bean (daizu): One of the most important foodstuffs in Japan, from which tofu, soya milk, yuba and soya oil are made, among others. Soya beans are a component of miso and soy sauce. They contain a lot of protein, which is broken down by koji mould to develop flavour-enhancing properties. There are many different varieties including round and black soya beans.

Soy sauce (shoyu): Soy sauce is a universal seasoning sauce that is high in umami flavour. It's made from cereals (mostly wheat), soya beans, water and salt fermented with koji mould. The two main varieties are dark (koikuchi) and light (usukuchi) soy sauce. The latter is saltier, but has a finer and lighter taste. A light-coloured and light-flavoured, non-pasteurised soy sauce is particularly suitable for our recipes.

Tofu: Tofu is made from coagulated soya milk. In Japan there are two types: the soft silken tofu (kinugoshidofu) and the firm, regular 'cotton' tofu (momendofu). Particular to Kyoto is a very fine tofu with a mild, rounded and sweetish flavour, which is often eaten on its own, seasoned only with soy sauce.

Wakame: This seaweed is an important component of miso soup. It is also sold in a dried and salted form. In the spring in Japan, wakame is often served fresh, only briefly blanched, and accompanied by bamboo shoots.

Yuba: Soya milk skin is an important component of Zen temple cuisine and a speciality of Kyoto, where it's available both fresh and dried. Yuba is very nutritious and has a fine, sweetish taste and a high protein content. It tastes best on its own seasoned only with a quality light soy sauce.

Many of these products, made by hand with high quality, are available at:www.mimiferments.com

REFERENCES

The following references inspired and guided us in our work on this book:

Andoh, Elizabeth: *Washoku. Recipes from the Japanese Home Kitchen*, Berkeley 2005

D¯ogen und Ko¯sho¯ Uchiyama Ro¯shi: *How to Cook Your Life*, Boston 2005

Fujii, Mari: *The Enlightened Kitchen. Fresh Vegetable Dishes from the Temples of Japan*, New York 2012

Jahn, Gisela, Petersen-Brandhorst, Anette: *Erde und Feuer. Traditionelle japanische Keramik der Gegenwart*, ('Earth and fire.Traditional Japanese Ceramics of the Present'), exhibition catalogue (Hetjens-Museum, Deutsches Museum und Museum für Völkerkunde Berlin), Munich 1984

Jullien, François: *Über das Fade – eine Eloge. Zu Denken und Ästhetik in China (In Praise of Blandness, Proceeding from Chinese Thought and Aesthetics)*, Berlin 1999

Koyama, Hirohisa: *Japan und seine Esskultur ('Japan and its Food Culture')*, Munich 1999

Murata, Yoshihiro: *Kaiseki*. Tokyo/New York 2006

Paul, Stevan: *Meine japanische Küche. Rezepte für jeden Tag ('My Japanese Cuisine. Everyday Recipes')*, Münster 2018

Suzuki, Tokiko: *Japanese Homestyle Cooking*, Tokyo 1999

Tsuji, Kaichi: *Kaiseki. Zen Tastes in Japanese Cooking*, Kyoto/Tokyo/Palo Alto 1972

Tsuji, Shizuo: *Japanese Cooking. A Simple Art*, New York/San Francisco 1980

Yoneda, Soei: *Good Food from a Japanese Temple. Six Hundred Year Tradition of Simple, Elegant Vegetable Cooking*, Tokyo/New York/San Francisco 1982

ACKNOWLEDGEMENTS

We would like to thank our families, Siddhartha, Noah and Solvej, as well as Meike and Floris, for giving us the spaces to create our cookbook, and to cook, write and take photographs in the Spree Forest.

Our thanks also go to our parents, who generously gave us their time and were there for the grandchildren, and to the inhabitants of the Spree Forest who accompanied us and made it possible to work on location.

We are very grateful for the support and inspiration received from ceramists Carolin Wachter (wachter-porzellan.de), Cuzé (studio-cuze.tumblr.com), Yoshito Maeoka and Gurli Elbækgaard (elbaekgaard.dk), and for the suggestions and products provided by Markus Shimizu (mimiferments.com). He produces the high-quality artisanal miso, soy sauces, sangohachi and mirin mentioned in the book in Germany. Thanks also go to Nicole Klauß for her reliable guidance during the creation of the book and her constructive criticism of texts and recipes. Thanks also go to Esther Kern, who supported us with her advice. We also thank Claudia Zaltenbach for the tip to soften yuba with baking soda (a taster of her next cookbook on tofu and yuba).

And last but not least, thanks to Urs Hunziker and his team at AT Verlag for their trust in us and our idea.

MALTE HÄRTIG

is a trained chef, researcher and writer of cookbooks and a philosopher. He wrote his PhD thesis on Japanese food culture and Zen Buddhism. He has a fondness for unusual ideas and appreciates the beauty and variety to be found in vegetables, cooking and thinking. He lives with his family in Germany's Wendland region.
www.malte-haertig.de

JULE FELICE FROMMELT

works as a freelance food photographer in Berlin. Her pictures aim to capture the essence and beauty of things. Her photographs have a natural and clean aesthetic. She loves uncomplicated food and photographs it that way. She likes to cook and eat vegetables from her own garden in the Spree Forest. She helped develop the recipes for this book.
www.julefelicefrommelt.de

RECIPE INDEX

Basic techniques

Published in 2020 by
Grub Street
4 Rainham Close
London
SW11 6SS

Email: food@grubstreet.co.uk
Web: www.grubstreet.co.uk
Twitter: @grub_street
Facebook: Grub Street Publishing

Copyright © AT Verlag 2019
Published originally in German as *Von Zen Und Sellerie*
Photography: Jule Felice Frommelt

A CIP catalogue record for this book is available from the British Library.

ISBN 978-1-911667-04-9

Printed and bound by Finidr, Czech Republic